Advance Praise for

DEATH FOR BEGINNERS

Your No-Nonsense, Money-Saving Guide to Planning for the Inevitable

"Practical, plain-spoken, helpful, and humorous, *Death for Beginners* guides the reader through the entire process of planning for death from 'what do I do with my body' to 'who do I leave out of my will.' By exploring funeral options, this book educates you about the funeral experience in a practical manner with good laughs along the way."

—R. Brian Burkhardt, author of *Rest in Peace*

"*Death for Beginners* is a delightful read about a very serious subject we all have to face eventually. Karen Jones has done a superb job of presenting the vast array of choices involved in making funeral arrangements. Her humor makes the necessities of this often taboo topic accessible, easy to grasp, and yes, fun. I have assisted dozens of families in making funeral arrangements, and every one of them would have benefitted from reading this book."

—Brian Flowers, Green Burial Council
National Advisory Board Member

DEATH FOR BEGINNERS

Your No-Nonsense, Money-Saving Guide to Planning for the Inevitable

by Karen Jones

Quill
Driver
Books

Fresno, California

Published by Quill Driver Books, an imprint of Linden Publishing
2006 South Mary, Fresno, California 93721
559-233-6633 / 800-345-4447
QuillDriverBooks.com
Quill Driver Books and Colophon are trademarks of
Linden Publishing, Inc.

Quill Driver Books titles may be purchased in quantity at special
discounts for educational, fund-raising, business, or promotional
use. Please contact Special Markets, Quill Driver Books, at the
above address or at 559-233-6633.

To order another copy of this book, please call
1-800-345-4447
ISBN 978-1-884995-61-3
135798642

Printed in the United States of America on acid-free paper.

Library of Congress Cataloging-in-Publication Data

Jones, Karen
  Death for beginners : your no-nonsense, money-saving guide to
planning for the inevitable / by Karen Jones.
      p. cm.
  Includes bibliographical references and index.
  ISBN 978-1-884995-61-3 (pbk. : alk. paper)
  1. Death--United States--Planning. 2. Death--Social aspects--
United States. 3. Funeral rites and ceremonies--United States--
Planning. I. Title.
  HQ1073.J66 2010
  306.90973--dc22
                                      2010006102

Mixed Sources
Product group from well-managed
forests and other controlled sources
www.fsc.org Cert no. SW-COC-002283
FSC © 1996 Forest Stewardship Council

Contents

This book is dedicated to the memory of Esther Jaria Willey.

Acknowledgments

Writing this book made me laugh out loud. Once I overcame the flutters about the topic, I jumped in and enjoyed myself. I cannot tell you how many times I have "dined out" on the stripper-casket story.

Trying to organize this amount of similar and overlapping information was a challenge. It was amazingly easy to become sidetracked. That said, I hope I accomplished what I set out to do.

I am grateful to the Funeral Consumers Alliance for the wealth of information it provided me. You should consider joining the local chapter in your area. These are good folks with great information and they are committed to just and fair burial practices.

Many thanks to the people who helped with the book. First, my agent Linda Konner, who flogged this horse for years until the bright, savvy, and discerning Quill Driver Books took notice. Thanks also to Ruth Fordon, who was my first reader, and to Mary Jeanne Ainsley who gave the book a thorough going-over before I handed it off to my editor. To all of my friends on Facebook, many thanks for the stories and encouragement.

Also, thanks to Jeanette Praz for the entertaining cremation container story, to Peter Baker, who came up with just the right words—"one step beyond insightful into inappropriate"—to James E. Hutchins, Esq., who reviewed the section on wills, to Matt Shea for the Drunken Pin the Tail on the Donkey giving game, to Kathleen Brehony, who found the YouTube clip of the trailer for *The Brain That Wouldn't Die*, and last, but not least, to my husband Steve, who, even though declaring that writing this book left me with no remaining social discourse, took me out to dinner anyway.

Return To Sender. The grave of Elvis Aaron Presley, Graceland Mansion Estates.

A First Note: Why Think About Death?

Hoping to catch the bus, nineteen-year-old Esther dashed across the street, only to be struck and thrown fifty yards by an oncoming pickup truck. She died three days later. The family was stunned and rendered helpless by the tragedy. Esther's sister, my best friend, Regina, pitched in to help with the decisions. What about organ donation? Would Esther have wanted that? Who should speak at the funeral? Wait, what about the service—what should be mentioned, what needed to be left out? I wanted to help but found myself completely useless. All I could do was spit out strange bits of advice like, "Be sure to wear waterproof mascara to the funeral." What list should that suggestion go on?

The fact was that there were no lists, no instructions. Esther's friends and family were flying blind, with grief and shock clouding their decisions. Tell me, just exactly how *do* you bargain for the best price on a cemetery plot when you are going to use that land to dig a hole and put your sister in it?

Because of Esther's death, this book was born. Watching Regina and her family deal with this unexpected tragedy made me determined that no one else should have to fumble their way through the dark night of grief. The loss itself is hard enough. But even worse, in the mad scramble to take care of details, wrong decisions are often made, money is wasted, feelings are hurt and stress is exponentially compounded. I wanted to help people create a road map for survivors to follow, a trail of breadcrumbs that would let friends and family know just what to do when "the time comes," a plan that would enable survivors to spend their time and energy on the things that truly matter.

Yes, Esther was only 19 and her tragic death was so completely unexpected that one could justify the lack of preparation. But stop for a minute. Down deep, do any of us really expect to die? We push it away. After all, the Lone Ranger was shot at many times and never bit the dust. Moose and Squirrel were constantly targeted by Boris and Natasha and yet they survived. Sky King never once fatally crashed his plane *Song Bird*. So clearly, we're immortal.

At least we think so. There are approximately 81 million Baby Boomers and we're pretty sure that despite what Jim Morrison said, we really *are* going to get out of here alive. While that might be a good feeling to carry around and cling to in the dark of night, the truth is that sooner or later we're all going to, as my Air Force colonel friend says, "mort." Every single one of us. Breathe deeply and remain serene.

MOM WOULD BE PROUD

As your dear old mom always said, be considerate of others. You don't want people running around frantically after your death, trying to pull together a funeral, do you?

What if they decide to have you buried, when you—having read way too many Edgar Allen Poe stories about scratch marks on the insides of coffin lids—wanted to be cremated? What if they plan a traditional, formal church service and you wanted a celebration on the beach with a bonfire and classic rock blaring from the 8-track? What if your hateful cousin sneaks that picture of you sporting a heinous 70s hairdo onto the memorial table? What if no one notifies that long-ago *special* friend? You know the one I'm talking about, right? Yeah, I thought so.

In the fine tradition of Daniel Boone, who forged the wilderness in his coonskin cap, it's time to make some plans. And this book is going to help. I've tried to make *Death for Beginners* a quick read, filled with lots of information you can get to fast. This book will help you plan what you want to have done after *you* die, and will help you if you find yourself in charge when a family member or close friend dies.

Each chapter contains a mix of facts, definitions, options, examples, pros and cons, costs, how to carry out your choices, things that are good to know, and websites with more information. At the back of the book are easy-to-use worksheets for you to photocopy, fill out, and give to whoever will be in charge of things for you. Also, at the end of the book are resources and checklists. As you read this book, you can visit **DeathForBeginners.com**, where you can download and print the worksheets at the back of the book, and click on the chapter-by-chapter links for further exploration of topics that interest you.

There. Take a breath. And while we're at it, let's take a break:

- Surviving members of the Grateful Dead, along with Jerry Garcia's friends and family, attended a private service in Tiburon, California, on August 11, 1995. In order to prevent Deadheads from mobbing the church, the location of the service was a closely guarded secret. Jerry was visible in an open casket, wearing a black t-shirt and a windbreaker. Floral decorations included thunderbolts made of roses. Garcia's daughter Annabelle, 25, is reported to have said what a lousy father he'd been, but smiled when she said it.

- In keeping with his image and his own view of himself as the ultimate playboy, Hugh Hefner purchased an ornate vault next to Marilyn Monroe's vault at the mausoleum in Westwood Memorial Park in California. Hefner thought it only fitting that he be laid to rest next to the other major sex icon of the twentieth century.

- Tired of the same old coffins? Crazy Coffins has a fine selection of alternatives, including coffins shaped like birdcages, ballet shoes, guitars, and—my personal favorite—gigantic wine corks. Check out **www.CrazyCoffins.co.uk**.

- And you don't want to miss the Celebrity Death Beeper—it e-mails you when a celebrity or sports figure dies. The website says it's "Free. Simple. Easy. Fun. Now checking for deaths every 10 minutes." **CelebrityDeathBeeper.com**

That wasn't so bad, was it? So get on with it. Remember when Dale and Roy wished us Happy Trails? They meant the *entire* trail, even the part that leads off into the sunset. Think of this book as a guide to that last stretch of your own, personal happy trails. Because, my friends, all of us are going to go riding into that cowboy sunset, and if the trail is well marked, those we've left behind will have an easier time of it.

How to Use this Book

You might want to read *Death for Beginners* with a highlighter in hand for easy future reference. You do not have to read the book in order, front to back, although it will help because, as I go along, I do reference information given previously so as to not repeat myself and bore you to tears. The worksheets at the back of the book tie all the information together into one streamlined package (but you'll understand the worksheets better if you read the book first!).

Two additional things:

- The prices quoted are intended to give you a general idea of what things cost. Most prices are based on late 2009 information. Many prices vary wildly across geographic location and among individual providers.

- The majority of websites listed that offer goods and services such as caskets, burial at sea, ashes sent up in fireworks, and so forth, have not been vetted by either me or this book's publisher, and my listing them is not meant to be an endorsement. These sites are offered for your interest and exploration. There are a few websites that I *do* recommend, and these are stated plainly in the text.

CHAPTER 1

Knocking on Heaven's Door: What to Do with Your Body

There he is. With a hump on his back and a dirty cloak swirling around his ankles, he's examining the brains floating in jars. Reading the labels, he mumbles, "Looks good to me," and, smiling, makes his choice. Turning to leave, he sees himself in a mirror and, startled, drops the jar. Quickly recovering, he shoves the scrambled brain under the table with his foot. Peering frantically at the remaining brains, he grabs the jar nearest to him and rushes out of the door.

Yikes! Do you want Igor stealing your body parts like he did in the movie *Young Frankenstein*? Wouldn't you rather have a say about where your parts will go? While today's choices of what to do with your body after death don't (or at least shouldn't) include the Transylvanian method, you might not want to take the chance.

So here we are at the first decision you need to make about this whole death business: What do you want done with your body? How do you want to be… uh… disposed of? It's best to decide your final destination *now*, because this will determine how your body should be handled immediately after death and what kind of funeral or ceremony you will have.

Basically, there are six different ways to get rid of a body—or parts of it. (Legally, that is—I'm not talking about stuffing it into a car trunk or throwing it in a river.) This chapter takes you through your choices:

Body Bequeathing (Aka Giving Your Body to Science)

If you like the idea of making the world a better place even after you're dead, you can bequeath your body to a medical school or scientific research facility. In the old days, this was called "Giving your body to science," which always makes me picture my family solemnly handing my corpse over to 1950s-era scientists in gleaming white lab coats.

There are two kinds of places which you can give your body to: a medical school or a body farm.

Medical Schools

When you donate your body to a medical school, it will most likely be used by medical students for gross anatomy (the study of the entire body). It may also be used for other classes, such as surgical anatomy, where doctors study specific areas of the body. Your body may also be used to help train licensed doctors in the study of new and innovative procedures.

Body Farms

When you donate your body to a body farm, it will be placed outdoors in a protected research facility and left to decompose under changeable environmental conditions. The data generated from your body will give real-life instruction to forensic anthropology students and researchers. The data will also provide crucial information to law enforcement officers as they calculate time and manner of death of murder victims. Just think, you could help catch a killer even after you are dead. Very cool.

There are four body farms in the United States: the Forensic Anthropology Center at the University of Tennessee, Knoxville, Tennessee; the Western Carolina Human Identification Laboratory at Western Carolina University in Cullowhee, North Carolina; the Southeast Texas Applied Forensic Science Facility at Sam Houston

State University, Huntsville, Texas; and the Forensic Anthropology Center at Texas State University, San Marcos, Texas.

Pros & Cons

- You might not want people messing with your body after you are dead.
- Your religion may not encourage or condone body bequeathal.
- This choice may upset those you leave behind.
- You will be doing something wonderful for science, truth, justice, and the American Way. I see Superman standing there in black and white with the flag waving behind him—don't you?

Costs

The major cost involved in body bequeathing is transporting the body from the place of death. If you donate your body to a medical school, the medical school will usually pay or reimburse these expenses.

If you donate your body to a body farm, the farm will usually pick up your body for free if you're within its area when you die. The University of Tennessee will pick your body up for free if you are within 200 miles of Knoxville. Western Carolina University will transport your body free of charge if the body is within 200 miles of Cullowhee. Sam Houston State University will arrange for transportation free of charge if you die within the state of Texas and within 200 miles of Huntsville. Texas State University will transport your body at no charge if you die within 100 miles of San Marcos. If you live (or die) farther away, you'll have to make arrangements before your death to have a funeral transport service transport your body, at your own cost.

Service

If you donate your body to a medical school, you can have a traditional funeral service (where your body attends as the guest of honor) or a memorial service (just like a funeral, except your body isn't there). The funeral director should contact the school before preparing the body to find out the school's preparation requirements. Following the service, the body will be transferred to the medical school rather than to a cemetery.

After the medical school is done using you for classes or research, there's still the small matter of the final disposal of your bodily remains. The medical school will dispose of your remains by cremation or return them to your family for burial or cremation. If you like, you can have your funeral or memorial service at that time, when your body is really, finally, laid to rest. Realize that this might take a couple of years depending on the academic cycle.

If you donate your body to a body farm, you can have either a memorial service or a service with the body present. The crucial thing is that you cannot be embalmed. (Remember, they're going to study how you decompose naturally.) Remains are not returned to the family. In the case of the Forensic Anthropology Center at the University of Tennessee, the skeletons are added to the William M. Bass Donated Skeletal Collection.

Tour the Body Farm

In this video, Dr. Bill Bass, coauthor of *Beyond the Body Farm*, takes the viewer on a tour of a body farm. He shows and discusses human remains, skin slippage, and DNA analysis. **YouTube. com/watch?v=GSDCiOW81mk**

How Do I Do It?

Contact the medical school or the forensic anthropology center of your choice. Now.

Potential donors are encouraged to establish files ahead of time. The respective body bequeathal programs will help with the forms and answer any questions.

4

Good to Know

- Donation to forensic anthropology centers and donation to some medical schools will not preclude organ/tissue donation. You can check on this when you make your arrangements.

- It's an excellent idea to let at least one person who is close to you know your wishes ahead of time. It might be a week or so before your will is read and that would defeat the purpose of the bequest. It's also a good idea for others to know beforehand, because this type of thing can be a shock to survivors.

- Both medical schools and forensic anthropology centers may decline donation depending on specific guidelines, some of which include refusal for death from infectious disease such as HIV, tuberculosis, hepatitis of any kind, or antibiotic resistant infections such as MRSA. Just in case, you should have alternative plans for the disposition of your body.

On the Web

- Anatomy Gifts Registry—AGR is a division of the Anatomic Gift Foundation, a non-profit organization founded in 1994 that helps with whole body donation and tissue donation. It is in compliance with the revised Uniform Anatomical Gift Act and has easy procedures to follow. **AnatomicGift.com**

- The Forensic Anthropology Center, at the University of Tennessee—This site is about their body farm. A fascinating read, even if this is not your choice. **Web.utk.edu/~fac**

- Revised Uniform Anatomical Gift Act—This site explains the law governing organ donations for the purpose of transplantation, and the law governing the making of anatomical gifts of one's cadaver to be dissected in the study of medicine. If you're interested, this is the last word on body donation. **www.law.upenn.edu/bll/archives/ulc/uaga/2006final.htm**

- Sam Houston State University—The Southeast Texas Applied Forensic Science Facility, Huntsville, Texas. **www.CJCenter.org/stafs/index.html**

- Texas State University—The Forensic Anthropology Center at Texas State University, San Marcos, Texas. **TXState.edu/anthropology/facts**

- Western Carolina University—The Western Carolina Human Identification Laboratory, Western Carolina University, Cullowhee, North Carolina. **WCU.edu/3409.asp**

Organ Donation

If handing your entire body over to medical science sets your teeth on edge or your elderly auntie would faint at the idea, you might want to consider organ donation. This way you help humanity but stop short of bequeathing your entire body. Much has been written about organ donation and its wonderful benefits. The Mayo Clinic states: "Enough people to populate a small city—nearly 100,000—are on the U.S. organ transplant waiting list, waiting for an organ donation. On an average day, about 77 people receive organ transplants." Organ donation is a good thing to do. I plan to do this. It's just too bad I can't donate fat cells right now.

With organ donation, the organs are removed in a process much like surgery and all incisions are closed after the procedure. A national computer network, the Organ Procurement and Transplantation Network, then matches donated organs with recipients throughout the country. Here's what you can donate:

- Organs: heart, lungs, kidneys, pancreas, liver, and intestines. Organs must be used between six and 72 hours after removal from the donor's body.

- Tissue: corneas, skin, veins, tendons, bone, bone marrow, heart valves, middle ear, brain, cartilage, ligaments, and connective tissue. Tissues can be preserved and stored in tissue banks for later use. Middle ear tissue can be donated for those with hearing loss and brain tissue can be donated for research into Alzheimer's disease, Parkinson's disease, and other related disease research.

- Stem Cells: marrow, peripheral blood stem cells, and cord blood stem cells.
- You can also donate your blood and blood platelets.

Pros & Cons

- This choice might upset those left behind, or your religious practice may not encourage this option.
- One person can save or enhance up to 60 lives through organ and tissue donation.
- Often families find a loved one's organ donation helps them through their grieving process. It's a good deal all the way around.

Costs

There is no cost to the donor's family. The recipient pays costs.

Service

Once your organs and tissue have been harvested, your body will be released, usually within 24 hours. You can then have any type of service you want, from a memorial service to a full funeral service. In the traditional funeral service, your body is clothed, so there is no sign of organ donation.

For eye donation, an artificial eye is inserted and the lids are closed. With bone donation, funeral directors use rods inserted where the bone was. As for skin donation, the skin is only taken from your back. No problem there.

How Do I Do It?

Organs cannot be stored and must be used within hours of removing them from the donor's body, so time is of the essence. Signing a Uniform Donor Card (one is provided in the resources section of this book) or noting your choice on your driver's license is the first step, but this does not guarantee that your organs will be donated. What if you die and no one can find your wallet? It's important to have your wishes recorded on the worksheets copied from the back of the book (or downloaded from **DeathForBeginners.com**) and in your will. But most important, let your family know your wishes, because hospitals will ask next of kin for permission.

Just think, you may give the gift of life after you're dead. How great is that?

Good to Know

- There is no cutoff age for organ donation. Organs have been successfully transplanted from donors in their seventies and eighties.

- Many religions encourage organ donation and see it as a charitable act.

- Remember, you can donate organs even if you are bequeathing your body to science.

- You can also donate specific anatomical gifts such as only eyes, blood, kidneys, liver, etc.

On the Web

- Donate Life America—This site lets you sign up for organ donation by state and even has family notification cards you can print or e-mail. **DonateLife.net**

- Life Source Organ and Tissue Donation—This site provides extensive discussion of religious beliefs regarding organ donation. **Life-Source.org/donation/religious-views.shtml**

- OrganDonor—This is the official U.S. government web site for organ and tissue donation. It lists criteria for donation, who can donate, types of donation, what can be donated, and gives a good primer on donation basics. **OrganDonor.gov**

Direct Disposition

There is some confusion about this term. Some say it involves only burial and others say it also involves cremation. I say let's go with both. My friend Kathleen, who was raised in New Jersey, would say this is the "bada boom bada bing" method. In general, direct disposition is the removal of the body from the place of death, placing it in a container or casket, and delivering it to the cemetery or crematorium without any attendant religious services or other rites or ceremonies.

> ## The Brain That Wouldn't Die
>
> This is a thrilling movie about a young transplant doctor who is experimenting with new techniques when his fiancé is decapitated in a car crash. Using his new skills he keeps her head alive while he searches for a new body. The 1962 movie trailer is on YouTube: **YouTube.com/watch?v=PYebuwQ8RPw.**

Pros & Cons

- Loved ones left behind might feel cheated of the opportunity to grieve at a ceremony.

- You will be dead and won't have to listen to them, will you?

- This choice is one of the most inexpensive of all options.

- This may be a good option if you are in charge of the old guy next door who has outlived all of his family and friends.

Costs

You will pay a fee for removal of the body from the place of death, including transportation to the cemetery or crematorium, Expect to pay for the container, shelter of the body prior to disposition, including refrigeration in lieu of embalming, external cleaning of the body, and possibly filing of necessary legal documents. There will also be charges for grave opening and closing and/or perpetual care (maintenance) of the gravesite. Costs will obviously be lower with cremation and the scattering of ashes.

Service

- If you want no service whatsoever, this may be the way to go.
- You can have a memorial service at a later date.
- A small bedside service can be held before the body is taken away.

How Do I Do It?

Call your funeral director now. He will make all of the prearrangements for you. Some states will allow a family member or friend to take your body from the place of death to the funeral home or crematorium, but you need to check first with your area medical examiner or your state's attorney general before you make this choice. Even then, the funeral director in charge of the actual burial or cremation might not allow it.

Good to Know

- Embalming is not required for the first 24 hours and in most states it is not required at all. Contrary to urban myth, there is no public health risk if the body is not embalmed.

On the Web

- The National Association of Attorneys General—To find the correct phone number to check if your state allows transportation of a body without a license, just click on the map and your attorney general's e-mail and phone number will be displayed. **Naag.org**

Self Service

Friends or family may take your body from the place of death in order to prepare it for a home or green burial, or a home service. This is often done by those who traditionally care for their dead without any assistance from funeral directors, such as some Mennonites and Quakers. In other cases, rural families, such as those in the Ozarks or Appalachian mountains, take care of their own family needs and have always done so. More recently, this is a choice made by those who have home burials or green burials (see Chapter 2 for more on green burials). More and more people are finding great comfort in caring for their loved ones themselves.

Pros & Cons

- This is a good option if you are more comfortable having your body taken care of by friends and family rather than by hired help.

- This option relies exclusively on the participation of family and friends. While it may be your choice, others may not be so excited about it.

Costs

The cost of transporting the body will be limited to things such as gas or van rental. You may need to buy a temporary license for this type of transportation.

Service

- You can have any type of service you want.

How Do I Do It?

First, you call your local medical examiner or your state's attorney general to find out if self-transportation and home preparation are options and, if so, obtain a list of any requirements. If you want to have your body prepared by family and friends but want to have a standard funeral rather than a home burial, a funeral service provider must be involved. You need to discuss their level of cooperation beforehand. If you wish to be cremated, check to determine what the requirements involved in getting the body to the crematorium are. Finally and most importantly, you need to have open and detailed discussions with your loved ones to decide who will do exactly what.

Good to Know

- More and more people are beginning to take an interest in home services and burials, and this practice is becoming increasingly accepted.

- There are many good sites on the Web to find useful information on how to execute this choice.

On the Web

- Final Passages—This excellent web site gives facts, definitions, and examples of aftercare: **www.NaturalDeathCare.org**.

- The Funeral Consumers Alliance—This specific Web address lists state laws concerning self-service: **Funerals.org/your-legal-rights/caring-for-your-own-dead**.

KEEP YOUR DNA

Did you know that some funeral homes are offering to retrieve and preserve a sample of your DNA? The service is being offered though a program at the Marshall University Forensic Science Center in West Virginia. The fee is about $150. DNA can be tested for the presence of genetic diseases as well as for paternity. It can also help trace ancestry. Who knows? One day a test might prove you were related to Princess Di. Learn more at the Marshall University Science Center website: **Forensics.Marshall.edu/MUFSC/default.html**.

Traditional Care

In the United States, it is traditional for your body to be taken from the place of death to a funeral home by a funeral service provider for preparation for burial or cremation with accompanying services.

Pros & Cons

- This method is probably the way to go if you are having a traditional funeral service.

- This choice is easy on those left behind.

- Traditional funerals can be very expensive—as are most things that we hand over to the care of others.

Costs

You will pay a fee for removal of the body from the place of death, a container in which to transfer the body, and the filing of the necessary legal documents. Once the body is on-site, other costs, such as dressing, casketing, embalming or disinfecting, equipment usage, staffing the visitation, and opening of the grave, will be accrued. More information on costs for traditional funerals can be found in Chapter 2.

Service

- Once your body is at the funeral home, you may choose any service they offer, including ones on-site or off-site.

How Do I Do It?

If this is the option you want, then it is best to go ahead and choose a funeral home now. You can use the recommendations of family and friends. You should also check a funeral home's website and your local Better Business Bureau. Narrow it down to two or three and pay each a visit.

Good to Know

- Do not Google "what to do with a dead body" unless you have a really strange sense of humor. You're going to go do that right now, aren't you?

On the Web

- The Funeral Consumers Alliance—This is the site of the oldest and largest national nonprofit funeral consumer advocacy organization in the country. It is the best place on the Web to obtain important information concerning all aspects of funerals. I strongly suggest you take a look at this site: **Funerals.org**.

- "How To Plan A Funeral": **EHow.com/how_3455_funeral.html**.

- "How to Plan an Affordable Funeral," Kimberly Palmer, *U.S. News & World Report*: **USNews.com/blogs/alpha-consumer/2007/10/17/how-to-plan-an-affordable-funeral.html**.

There is one other way to dispose of your body. It is unusual—to say the least—and may have you singing M-I-C-K-E-Y. Why? Because we like you....

CRYONICS

Being quick-frozen was good enough (cold enough, too?) for Ted Williams and, rumor has it, Walt Disney. Actually, the Uncle Walt rumor is false according to Snopes.com. I know, it was fun to believe, wasn't it? Now, regarding baseball's Ted Williams, I'll simply refer you to this CBS News report: "Ted Williams Frozen in Two Pieces: Meant to Be Frozen in Time; Head Decapitated, Cracked, DNA Missing" (**CBSNews.com/stories/2002/12/20/national/main533849.shtml**).

According to the Alcor Life Extension Foundation, located in Scottsdale, Arizona, cryonics is "the science of using ultra-cold temperature to preserve human life with the intent of restoring good health when technology becomes available to do so." Sounds good, like something Mr. Spock would approve of. The procedure involves replacing much of the water in the body's cells with chemicals that do not freeze. To qualify, the individual must have a viable brain and be legally deceased by cardiac death.

Pros & Cons

- Waking up in the future, fully cured, is a terrific idea.

- The technology does not yet exist to reverse the cryonics process. It is hoped that nanotechnology will offer answers. But until then, you remain "frozen" until technology can catch up with you. So there is no real chance of finally hooking up with that old girlfriend—unless, of course, she happens to choose the deep freeze too.

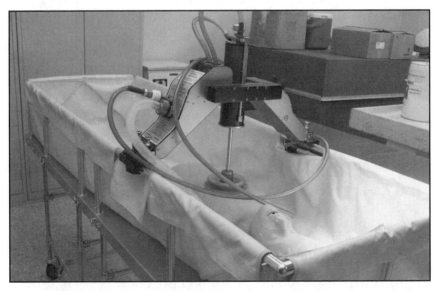

Preserve yourself for when that miracle cure comes along: the ice bath with a dummy in the prep room at the Cryonics Institute. *Photo courtesy of the Cryonics Institute (Cryonics.org)*

Costs

Costs vary widely among cryonics organizations. Alcor states that whole body preservation begins at $150,000. For preservation of the brain only—neuropreservation—the price begins at $80,000. The Cryonics Institute quotes a price of $28,000 for whole-body preservation but does not offer neuropreservation. The American Cryonics Society offers whole body preservation for $155,000 but declines to offer neuropreservation. With all of these organizations, you will also have to pay annual dues and there are surcharges for out-of-country participation. They encourage people who are interested in cryonics to investigate life insurance policies, trusts, and annuities as methods to come up with the moola.

Service

- Any service will have to be a memorial service, as the body must ideally begin the cryopreservation process within the first fifteen minutes of death.

How Do I Do It?

All cryonics organizations require you to fill out an application for membership that includes information about how you will fund your placement with them.

Good to Know

- If you are interested, just Google the term "cryonics" and you will receive a wealth of information. There are plenty of cryonics societies with different membership pricing rates.

- There are both nonprofit and for-profit cryonics businesses.

- You do not have to preserve your entire body. You can just preserve your head, so when the time comes, you can choose a new body. Let's all just spend a moment thinking about the kind of body we would choose.

On the Web

- The Alcor Life Extension Foundation—This site gives information about cryonics and states that it "is the world leader in cryonics, cryonics research, and cryonics technology." **Alcor.org**

- The American Cryonics Society—Established in 1969, this is the oldest U.S. cryonics society. The site features the informative article "Freeze A Jolly Good Fellow" at this website: **AmericanCryonics.org**.

- The Cryonics Society—An "unbiased, unaffiliated independent non-profit organization dedicated to advancing public understanding and scientific acceptance for this new emerging technology." This site has great links: **CryonicsSociety.org**.

- Cryonics Meetup Groups—This site provides a map for you to find people in your local area with whom you can discuss the pros and cons of cryonics: **Cryonics.Meetup.com**.

DEATH OVERSEAS

If you die outside of the country you live in, transporting your body will be unbelievably expensive. The worksheet at the end of this book gives you the choice of being cremated at the place of death and having your ashes shipped home.

HELP ME CHOOSE

Which of the following statements are true for you?

- I want to help science find cures and help physicians find better ways of healing.

- I'd like to try to save someone's life.

- I can be buried or cremated just fine without all of my organs.

- I don't want anyone messing with my body after I'm dead.

- I want to take all of my parts with me into the hereafter.

- It would be just fine to be taken from where I die to the funeral home or crematorium.

- I'd really like my family to be involved with taking my body where it needs to go.

- You know what? Just hire someone to take care of my body.

- I've got the money to be frozen until I can be revived and given a healthy new body.

CHAPTER 2

Break On Through to the Other Side: Slip Siding into the Ground

Here we examine burial—being placed into the ground (!). It might give you the willies, but stop for a minute and think. The tradition of being placed softly into the ground and lovingly covered up, just like your grandparents and their parents before, might not be so bad. Tradition is a strong source of comfort when dealing with the uneasy subject of death, and nowhere is tradition more marked than with a "proper burial."

My aunt likes to occasionally go to my grandmother's grave, have morning coffee, and read the newspaper. Friends of mine visit our mutual friend Robert's grave on Halloween and decorate it. This sounds strange until you know that he died on that night, in costume no less. It was his favorite holiday. We always wonder what Saint Peter thought when Robert showed up at the Pearly Gates dressed as half-businessman, half-surfer dude.

A lot of people like the idea of returning to dust, as it is said in the Bible. Even more people like the idea of becoming one with the earth, helping to nourish it. I have a friend who wants to be buried beneath an apple tree on her farm so that future generations can have a bite of her each summer. There's a joke there—I'm just not sure where.

In this chapter we will discuss the ways you can go sliding into the ground with a full-body burial. Cremation, with your ashes being placed in the ground, will be discussed in Chapter 3. Even if you've already decided on cremation, go ahead and give this chapter a read. After all, who can resist reading about the guy who was buried in his lounge chair with the key to his tomb in his pocket? See? You *just* have to keep reading now.

The type of burial you choose will involve several things:

- the kind of coffin you want
- the kind of ceremony you are interested in
- and the location.

For instance, you might want a kite-shaped coffin, complete with tail, or you might want to be placed in your 1968 Mustang—either choice making a traditionally-shaped burial plot a bit of a problem. (A full discussion about coffins can be found in Chapter 4.)

You might want your graveside ceremony to include a live, dancing, naked Elvis. If so, you could find it difficult to be buried near Jim Morrison, Edith Piaf, and Frederic Chopin in the historically-reserved Pere Lachaise Aris cemetery in Paris. However, Paris is Paris and Parisians can be quite ahead of the curve in these matters.

Maybe you want to be buried in a forest where you can literally return to the earth. There are conservation-type burials available for just that. Or perhaps burial at sea appeals to you so you can sleep with the fishes.

We've lots to choose from, so let's get started.

There are six different basic types of full body burial:

- traditional in-ground burial
- traditional entombment
- green or natural burial
- burial at sea
- home burial
- alternative burial.

Traditional in-Ground Burial

In a traditional burial, you have a regular coffin, use a by-the-book funeral home, get buried in a standard cemetery, and—usually—have a conventional ceremony. You have two choices with a traditional in-ground burial:

- interment, which is burial in the earth
- entombment, where your body is placed in an underground lawn crypt.

Pros & Cons

- If you are a person who values tradition, this is likely the burial option you want to do.
- It often will give comfort to your loved ones who may need a familiar ritual to help with the mourning process, and it will give them a place to visit over the years.
- In-ground burial is a good choice if a family plot is available.
- A traditional burial is usually the most expensive choice.

Costs

According to AARP.org, the average cost of a basic traditional funeral is close to $6,000, but spending $10,000 is not unusual.

Yeah, I gulped at those figures too. But it all depends upon your outlook. Actual prices are all over the map—literally, there are dramatic differences between geographical areas and among funeral providers in any given area. With a traditional in-ground burial, you will be paying for some or all of the following:

- Basic services: $990–$2,955—this is the base cost. To this, add the following:
- Coffin: $450–$47,000 (!)
- Transfer of the body from the place of death to the funeral home: $160–$395

- Receiving remains from another funeral home: $895–$3145
- Sending remains to another funeral home: $895–$3860
- Equip and staff graveside: $200–$695. This should include interment equipment, tent, chairs, etc.
- Dressing/casketing: $160–$490
- Embalming: $380–$675
- Disinfecting without embalming: $95–$295
- Visitation/viewing: $175–$490
- Ceremony at funeral home: $400–$640
- Hearse: $175–$400
- Limo: $185–$400

Additional costs may include the following:

- Plot or crypt in mausoleum
- Markers or monuments
- Vault or vault liner and installation
- Restoration of area after interment service
- Removal and disposal of funeral decorations
- Recording of cemetery documents
- Opening and closing of the grave
- Death certificate
- Obituary—writing and placement in newspaper
- Print package—including a register book, memorial cards or prayer cards, and acknowledgment cards
- Church or clergy stipend

As you can see, there are many charges you probably haven't thought about. It's a lot like buying a car. Who really thinks about all of those extra charges until you are signing the paperwork?

Where Is Ulysses S. Grant Buried?

The "Find A Grave" website can help you locate graves of thousands of people, including the famous. Here you can search around the world to locate ancestors and enemies. Searches can be made by surname, social security number, date of death, location, and more. Find A Grave boasts it will search 39 million grave records: **FindAGrave.com**.

The Burial Vault and Burial Liner

A burial vault is a strong, sealed box designed to protect the enclosed coffin. It is primarily used to keep the weight of the earth and cemetery equipment from crushing the coffin and to prevent the ground from sinking in. A burial liner covers only the top and sides of the coffin.

The cost of a liner or vault can range anywhere from $400 to $10,000. Very few states require a liner or vault. Some cemeteries require them to help keep maintenance costs low. If you don't want to have a vault or liner, look for a cemetery that does not require one.

Service

- Usually, you would have a traditional service. It can be as simple or elaborate as you wish and held anywhere, including at a place of worship, at a funeral home, or at the gravesite.

- Traditional burial is not the likely choice if you want a service that is unconventional or far outside of the norm.

Cemeteries

Your choice of cemetery will depend on your religious affiliation, personal preference, and the costs associated with each.

There are five basic types of cemeteries:

- National cemetery: Owned by the government and used for the interment of veterans and their dependents
- Public nonprofit cemetery: Owned and operated by a city or county
- Religious cemetery: Owned by a religious group; used specifically for those of that particular religion or faith
- Commercial cemetery: Owned and operated by a for-profit business
- Family cemetery: One that is located on private land.

There are three types of spaces:

- A grave is a single burial space.
- A plot is an area that contains more than one grave.
- A lawn crypt is a raised area of land where crypts, or underground burial chambers, are pre-installed.

You need to consider:

- If you want room for others to be buried near you
- If you want to be buried in consecrated ground
- If the location is important so that family and friends can easily visit
- If a preneed purchased plot or gravesite can be resold if you decide not to use it (very important!).

TRADITIONAL ENTOMBMENT

With a traditional entombment, you can go with the traditional coffin/ traditional funeral home route, but your casket is placed in a concrete enclosure known as a crypt. Your choices are:

- Being placed in the previously mentioned underground lawn crypt
- Being placed above ground in a mausoleum, which is a free-standing building constructed as a monument with individual crypts for interment
- Being placed in a chamber under your place of worship.

In August of 2009, the crypt above Marilyn Monroe's crypt went up for bid on eBay with a starting price of $500,000. The seller noted, "The person occupying the address right now is looking face down on her." So many jokes, so little space.

Pros and Cons

- Entombment is a good choice if you want your body to remain above ground but still want a full body burial.
- Cemetery mausoleums are out of the weather, well lit, and visitor friendly.
- This is a good choice if your family already has a mausoleum.

Costs

Entombment might seem to be a more cost-effective alternative to ground burial, but most of the basic costs are the same, since you need to purchase a crypt. The opening and closing costs for above ground crypts are lower because they involve less labor.

Service

- You can have any type of service you want. The typical service for entombment is a traditional one.

How Do I Do It?

- If you are considering traditional burial or entombment, it is critical that you do your research so you get what you want at a price you want. Contact your local Funeral Consumers Alliance. They provide a wealth of information.
- Research the various funeral homes in your area. Feel free to visit as many as you want and comparison shop.
- Use the Internet to comparison shop.
- Decide how you will pay for this burial option.

TRADITIONAL BURIAL FOR VETERANS

The Department of Veterans Affairs states that veteran burial benefits include a gravesite in a national cemetery, if there is space; opening and closing of the grave; perpetual care; a government headstone or marker; a burial flag; and a Presidential Memorial Certificate, at no cost to the family. Veterans may also be eligible for burial allowances. Some burial benefits are available for spouses and dependents. For a complete listing of benefits and requirements, visit the U.S. Department of Veterans Affairs—**www.Cem.va.gov/cem/bbene_burial.asp**.

Good to Know

- The Federal Trade Commission regulations state that all funeral-related charges must be itemized, printed on a general price list, and made available to the public by phone, by mail, or in person.

- A single grave can, in most cases, accommodate two caskets, one deeper than the other.

- Usually, different types of gravesites are available, depending on the marker you wish to place:

  - lots where only flat, ground-level markers are permitted

  - upright monument lots

  - lots for pillow markers (monuments with an elevated back, giving a sloped effect).

On the Web

- AARP—This link takes you to a good article about funeral costs: **Bulletin.AARP.org/yourmoney/personalfinance/articles/_the_high_costdy_ng.html.**

- The Federal Trade Commission—This website lists funeral regulations: **FTC.gov/bcp/menus/consumer/shop/funeral.shtm.**

- The Funeral Consumer Guardian Society—The FCGS is an independent consumer advocate organization for seniors, serving thousands of Americans. It has a section where you can estimate traditional funeral costs: **FuneralConsumer.org/estimate.html.**

- Funeral Ethics—Site for ethical issues, funeral regulations, and good information for the general pubic: **www.FuneralEthics.org.**

- National Funeral Directors Association—Site provides information about average funeral costs: **NFDA.org/about-funeral-service/trends-and-statistics.html.**

GREEN OR NATURAL BURIAL

...I bequeath myself to the dirt to grow from the grass I love,
If you want me again look for me under your boot-soles...
—"Song of Myself" by Walt Whitman

Green or natural burial is rapidly becoming one of the most popular types of burial. The green burial movement began in Great Britain in the mid-1990s, when people became concerned about pollution caused by cremation and embalming. With green or natural burial, the body is prepared for burial without chemical preservatives; it is put in a biodegradable container, either a casket or a shroud, and is placed in the earth to decompose naturally. Talk about getting rid of your carbon footprint!

This is the way most of our ancestors cared for their dead for thousands of years up until the late nineteenth century. Daniel Boone would approve.

It is interesting to note that, according to **NaturalBurial.org**'s FAQ page, each year in the United States' 22,500 cemeteries we bury roughly:

- 827,060 gallons of embalming fluid

- 90,272 tons of steel (caskets)

- 2,700 tons of copper and bronze (caskets)

- 1,636,000 tons of reinforced concrete (vaults)

- 14,000 tons of steel (vaults).

The Centre for Natural Burial states that "A ten-acre swatch of cemetery ground will contain enough coffin wood to construct more than 40 homes, nearly a thousand tons of casket steel, and another twenty thousand tons of concrete for vaults." Yeowsa!

Types of Green or Natural Burial

- Partial or hybrid burial can take place at a conventional cemetery if the cemetery will allow it. You can be buried without a vault and in a green manner. But, while your body will decompose naturally, the grounds above are generally maintained with herbicides, pesticides, and other eco-unfriendly types of care.

- A "natural burial ground" is a cemetery that endeavors to protect the environment. A natural burial ground often uses grave markers that don't intrude on the landscape. Irrigation, pesticides, and herbicides are not used. Often, native trees, shrubs, and flowers are planted on or near the grave to help protect wildlife.

- A "conservation burial ground," which is the greenest alternative, is a cemetery dedicated to ecological restoration and landscape-level conservation. It goes one step further than the natural burial ground in that it has an established conservation organization as a long-term warden. This type of burial helps to conserve land through zero degradation of existing wild areas and by providing habitat for native fauna.

Pros & Cons

- This would be your final eco-friendly act.
- Environmentally, it is the right thing to do.
- There is a nice "ashes to ashes, dust to dust" synchronicity about returning to the earth.
- Natural burial cemeteries can be hard to find.
- The idea of actually decomposing can be a bit creepy to some.

Costs

One thing to consider is that the money you pay for this service is helping to protect a green space instead of paying for upkeep of an artificial area filled with ecologically unfriendly containers and chemicals. Just a thought.

You will pay for the plot of land, the opening and closing of the grave, the marker, and perpetual care. Other costs include those listed previously in the traditional burial section, depending on how elaborate a ceremony you wish to have. The main difference in the cost is that you can certainly pay much less for a biodegradable casket (think homemade pine coffin or shroud), you will not have the embalming costs, and you definitely won't have to buy a vault.

Costs will differ depending on the level of conservation. For example, the White Eagle Memorial Preserve—a conservation burial ground—is a twenty-acre cemetery set within 1,300 wild acres of permanently protected land near the Columbia River Gorge National Scenic Area in Washington State.

The preserve's 2009 prices are:

- $2,200 for a 20-foot x 20-foot gravesite (there's a 15 percent discount for the second or third site)

- $1,450 receiving fee for the local funeral home

- $220 (10 percent of the gravesite) charge by law for the Endowment Care Fund

White Eagle Memorial Preserve ceremonialist Jade Sherer leads a large funeral procession out to the burial site. *Photograph by Logan Price, courtesy of White Eagle Memorial Preserve (NaturalBurialGround.com)*

- $600 for the opening and closing of each grave, including planting native plants on the gravesite, watering for the first year, and monitoring into the future

- $500 for the burial of cremated remains in an urn—which includes the cost of a small site

- A $250 donation is requested for cremated remains to be scattered along the canyon edge.

Service

- You can have any type service you wish, from a formal religious ceremony to a simple blessing.

- One thing to consider is the type of site. Some sites are configured like ordinary cemeteries, lending themselves to chairs and tents. Other cemeteries such as the conservational burial cemeteries are designated nature preserves where the ground is kept in its natural state. Ninety-four-year-old Aunt Sudie might have a hard time climbing over tree roots. As entertaining as that might be, especially if you particularly didn't like Aunt Sudie, it is something to think about when you explore the different sites.

TO EMBALM … OR PERHAPS NOT

If you are undecided about this option, here's something that may help you make up your mind: Take a look at the book *Grave Matters: A Journey through the Modern Funeral Industry to a Natural Way of Burial*, by Mark Harris (Scribner, 2007, 2008). Read the chapter titled "The Embalming of Jenny Johnson." Whoo boy! It's an eye-opener for sure. Grave Matters: **www.GraveMatters.us**.

How Do I Do It?

- The Centre for Natural Burial (web site listed below) is a good place to start to look for sites nearest you. You will want to make sure a potential site is certified and meets all state laws.

- Check with the Green Burial Council (web site address follows) for certified sites. Its natural burial grounds are required to have a deed restriction to ensure that a current green cemetery remains so in the future. Green Burial Council conservation burial grounds are required to have a conservation easement held by an established land trust.

Good to Know

- A certified natural burial cemetery is protected in two ways. Easements and legislation protect these sites perpetually from development, preventing future owners from using the site for a new mall.

- If the markers are small or not allowed, visitors use handheld GPS systems to locate the graves.

- Conservation burial sites limit visitation to sensitive areas.

- There are no federal laws and few state laws requiring embalming.

- There are no state or federal laws requiring the use of a vault.

- The manufacturing and transporting of vaults utilizes a tremendous amount of energy and contributes to 1.6 tons of reinforced concrete being produced. This would be avoided if everyone chose a green burial.

On the Web

- The Centre for Natural Burial—This site discusses natural burial and helps you find natural burial sites in your area. It also has state-by-state listing of burial laws.
  NaturalBurial.coop/USA

- Grave Matters—A list of the newest natural cemeteries with continual updating. **Grave-Matters.blogspot.com/2008/08/ newest-natural-cemeteries.html**

- Green Burial Council—Provides the latest information concerning green burial, is up on current legislation, and can help you find green burial sites. **GreenBurialCouncil.com**

- Memorial Ecosystems—This site discusses conservational burial. You can check out two of their locations: the Ramsey Creek Preserve in Westminster, South Carolina, and the Honey Creek Woodlands on the grounds of the 2,100-acre Monastery of the Holy Spirit near Conyers, Georgia. **MemorialEcosystems.com/ConservationBurial/tabid/110/Default.aspx**

- The Natural Burial Company—This website has a list of natural burial/cemetery options in North America. **NaturalBurialCompany.com**

Burial at Sea

If you decide to have a full body burial at sea, you will be joining the fine tradition of the many Norsemen who were set adrift on ships, and James Bond, who received a traditional Anglican burial at sea in *You Only Live Twice*. Yes, his death was faked, but you get the idea. The majority of burials at sea involve cremation, and we will discuss this in Chapter 3. For this chapter, full body burial at sea is defined as the disposing of human remains in the ocean, normally from a ship or boat. It is a traditional method of disposition that has been around for thousands of years.

Pros & Cons

- Full body burial at sea has many restrictions. The Environmental Protection Agency has strict guidelines and reporting procedures.

- Services on a boat during commitment are determined by sea and weather conditions. Some people get seasick. Some trips get cancelled due to storms.

- For some, this is a difficult choice because there is no marker at which to grieve.

- This is a good idea if you are eligible for a full body burial at sea by the U.S. Navy.

- If you are committed to this type of burial, your having gone to your final rest exactly as you wanted can be a great source of comfort to those left behind.

Costs

Full body at sea burial requires special preparation such as special marine coffins or a weighted body bag or piece of sailcloth. You may have to use the services of a funeral home and may also be required to engage the services of a maritime funeral director. Wintertime rates for sea burial are usually higher because of sea conditions. (This is tough to plan for.)

You will pay the cost of preparation, coffin, and transportation to the vessel. Costs may also include the traditional funeral costs, if desired, such as preparing the deceased for viewing and a ceremony. There will be a cost for the vessel and the captain and crew.

These costs are somewhat offset by the fact that you will not be paying for a vault grave liner, opening and closing of the grave, and perpetual care.

Costs vary depending on how elaborate you want the service, if you want family and friends on the boat, and so forth. New England Burials at Sea quotes $7,500 for a private four-to-six-hour cruise with committal and a service. Sea Services (**SeaServices. com**), another maritime funeral provider, estimates that a full body at sea burial is approximately two to three times as expensive as that of a traditional funeral with cemetery burial.

Service

You can have the service be as traditional or nontraditional as you want, but where the service takes place is the critical factor.

- Services can be held directly on the boat while the body is commended to the deep.

- Services can be held dockside or on the shoreline.

- You can have the body commended to the deep and then hold a memorial service.

How Do I Do It?

- It is important to plan this option prior to need. The first step is to research maritime funeral services on the Internet. Go to discussion forums and see what people have to say about specific providers. Be sure to compare costs and check with your Better Business Bureau.

- The next step is to find a business that specializes in full body at sea burials. There are many that will scatter cremation remains but only a few that undertake a full body commitment. Again, it is critical that you thoroughly investigate these businesses. The one you choose will have information regarding EPA rules and reporting, the local health department rules, and a list of good funeral providers.

- If you want to do it yourself, you will need a certificate of death from the medical examiner, approval from the health department, an appropriate coffin, and knowledge of EPA requirements and proper reporting.

Good to Know

- California is the only state that doesn't permit full body sea burials. The Environmental Protection Agency allows it but the California Health Department, which governs funeral homes, does not.

- The Environmental Protection Agency regulations state that the burial "shall take place at least three nautical miles from land and in water at least 600 feet deep. Certain areas, including east central Florida, the Dry Tortugas, Florida, and the area west of Pensacola, Florida, to the Mississippi River Delta, require water at least 1,800 feet deep. All necessary measures shall be taken to ensure that the remains sink to the bottom rapidly and permanently."

- Written notice must be given to your regional EPA office within 30 days of burial at sea.

- Inland water burials are regulated by the Clean Water Act. A permit is required from the appropriate state agency.

UNITED STATES NAVY BURIAL AT SEA PROGRAM

You can have a full body burial at sea by the United States Navy if you are: an active-duty member of the uniformed services, a retiree or veteran who was honorably discharged, a U.S. civilian Marine personnel of the Military Sealift Command, or a dependent family member of active duty personnel, retiree, or veteran of the uniformed services.

The ceremony is performed by the commanding officer of the ship and is done while the ship is deployed. This means that family members are not allowed to be present. Services are usually videotaped for the family. After the ceremony, the commanding officer will notify the family regarding the date, time, and longitude. You will have to pay for body preparation, coffin, and transportation of the body to the ship. To get started, you need to fill out a request form. These forms and other information can be found at the United States Navy Mortuary Affairs Burial at Sea Program website: **www.Navy.mil/navydata/questions/burial. html**. You can also call the United States Navy Mortuary Affairs office toll-free at 1-866-787-0081.

On the Web

- Environmental Protection Agency—List of requirements for full body burial at sea. **EPA.gov/region4/water/oceans/burial.htm**.

- NationMaster—An Internet encyclopedia listing religions that support burial at sea. **NationMaster.com/encyclopedia/Buried-at-sea#Modern_burial_at_sea_procedures**

Returning to the sea can be tranquil and memorable. This eco-friendly Atlantic Sea Burial Shroud with hand-poured ballast weights is used on customized full body sea tribute burial cruises held year round. *Photograph courtesy of NewEnglandBurialsatSea.com*

HOME BURIAL

Burying a deceased loved one on the family property was common until the mid-1900s. In Chapter 5, we will discuss home funerals. Home burial is less popular today, but it is still practiced. There are now death midwives, people who guide a family through the process, including burial and healing. Take a look at the following website for more information: **ThresholdsOfLife.org**.

Pros & Cons

- The nice part about this is you will be buried where you belong.
- Home burial is like simply returning to your family (but not having to listen to them).
- There are many rules and regulations with which you will have to comply.
- Guidelines and regulations are difficult to ferret out.

Costs

The costs will vary depending on how many regulations you must follow. In some states, you may be allowed to bury the body with just a simple death certificate and an appropriate piece of land. In other states, you will be required to have the body handled by a funeral home and there are restrictions on the types of caskets allowed. I know, you'd think it would be a matter of complete choice, right?

Service

- Since this is your land, there should be no restrictions on the type of service you hold.

How Do I Do It?

Home burial is allowed in most parts of the country but each state, and sometimes-differing localities within the state, have specific requirements and restrictions. You need to do your homework well beforehand. Requirements may include: having to use a funeral director, owning a certain amount of acreage, a plan for care of the land in perpetuity, a release from the health department so you can have the body, papers from the medical examiner which may include a burial transit permit, a permission-to-bury form, and a death certificate.

Even if you do not have to use a funeral director, you still have to follow all state laws that govern burial. The best resource for information regarding state laws is Lisa Carlson's *Caring for the Dead*: **UpperAccess.com/experts/Carlson.html**.

Good to Know

- There is no state or federal law that states that a body must be buried in a casket. How about that?

- There appears to be no single site as yet on the Internet that lists specific home burial requirements state-by-state. You can waste a good amount of time surfing the Web for this information. It is likely easier to call your local medical examiner.

- The home burial trend is gaining momentum in America and there are plenty of good places to start your research on the Web.

- In January 2009, Joshua Slocum, executive director of the Funeral Consumers Alliance, wrote an excellent article discussing the difficulties of home burial. He says that in seven states (CT, IN, LA, MI, NE, NY, UT), families are required to use a funeral home for "everything from filing the death certificate, to transporting the casket, to getting the body released from the hospital. Whether the family wants to hire a funeral director or not, whether they can afford to pay one or not." If this is a choice you are considering, I encourage you to read the entire article. You can find it at the Funeral Consumers Alliance website: **Funerals.org/newsandalerts/consumer-alerts/471-caringownlynchresponse**.

- If you decide to go this route, you will need to consider things such as how to keep the body cool in lieu of embalming and other after-death care challenges. A good place to start researching this information is at the website **Crossings.net**.

- You should call your local medical examiner's office and see what regulations are in effect. A call to your state's attorney general might yield further information.

On the Web

- Crossings—This is a home funeral and green burial resource center. **Crossings.net**

- Home Funeral Directory—resources and information about home burial. **HomeFuneralDirectory.com**

- PBS—The site for Elizabeth Westrate's PBS film *A Family Undertaking*, about the home burial movement. **PBS.org/pov/pov2004/afamilyundertaking**

Can You Hear Me Now?

According to funeral directors, a request that is becoming more and more frequent is for people to be buried with their cell phones. It seems like everyone wants to stay in touch—even from the grave. MSNBC quotes Ed Defort, publisher of *American Funeral Director*, as saying that this is a distinct trend: "I've even heard of cases where people are being buried with their iPod. Or one guy who was prepared for his viewing with his Bluetooth earphone in his ear."

This gives a whole new meaning to "catch you later."

Alternative Burial

This is where we get to lighten things up a bit. Remember the guy buried in his recliner? Here we go.

- In 1899, Reuben John Smith of Buffalo, New York, was buried in his upholstered, russet-leather recliner with a checkerboard placed on his lap. He was dressed warmly with a hat and a coat and had the key to his tomb in his coat pocket.

- Sam Jones lived on Ocracoke Island, North Carolina, during the 50s, 60s, and 70s. A colorful businessman, he contributed greatly to the small island's economy. In 1977, Mr. Jones died and was buried beside his beloved pony, Ikey D, on Springer's Point. Legend has it that Ikey D was buried standing up.

You too can be buried beside your best friend. The graves of Ikey D and Sam Jones, Ocracoke Island, NC. *Photo courtesy of Images by Ruth (IslandPath.com)*

- Harry "The Horse" Flamburis, former president of the Northern California Hells Angels in the mid-1970s, was found, along with his girlfriend, bound and shot, execution-style. He was buried in Cypress Lawn Cemetery outside of San Francisco. Two months later, members of the Hell's Angels returned to bury his adored Harley-Davidson on top of him. There's no word on what happened to the girlfriend's body.

- Mummification is forever. If you are interested in becoming a mummy—and I am not kidding about this—modern mummification is available through funeral homes worldwide. Summum's Mummification of Transference service will mummify you, starting at only $67,000 (**Summum.org/mummification**).

The Funeral Rule?

The Federal Trade Commission, the U.S. consumer protection agency, has developed the "Funeral Rule," which sets guidelines for the funeral industry. The Funeral Rule, in part, states:

- You are not required to purchase a "package" of goods and services from a funeral home.

- Funeral directors are required to give you pricing information on the phone if you ask for it.

- The mortuary cannot demand your name, address, or phone number before giving you the prices.

- Funeral homes must give you an itemized list of all the services and merchandise sold by the home and the associated costs, if asked.

- For a service that is required by law, the funeral home must give you a written explanation of the law before charging you.

- The funeral home must provide you with a list of the items you've chosen and the total cost of the arrangements before you pay.

- No federal law requires embalming. Some states require that a body be embalmed or refrigerated if it is not buried or cremated in a certain amount of time or if it is to cross state lines for burial. Refrigeration is less expensive.

Preneed

While preplanning is wise, especially with something that can be as costly as a traditional funeral, prepayment is fraught with traps for the unwary. Some preneed plans will not reimburse your money in full if you change your mind, and some are only required to provide "like services" for those contracted. Every state has different guidelines. The following URL has an excellent article prepared by the Funeral Consumers Alliance about the pitfalls of preneed: **Funerals.org/frequently-asked-questions/198-preneedpitfalls**.

Memorial Societies

Memorial societies are nonprofit consumer groups whose purpose is to help members obtain the best financial deal for a funeral through advance planning. They do not offer funeral services but negotiate for services at what they believe is a reasonable cost. Members receive discounts with certain providers, help with comparison shopping, and a wealth of funeral planning information.

There are about 150 memorial societies in the United States. There is usually a one-time fee to join and, perhaps, a records fee. Some memorial societies have a very small annual fee. Volunteers do most of the work and this helps keep costs down.

MARK TWAIN

About a politician who had recently died, Mark Twain wrote: "I did not attend his funeral; but I wrote a nice letter saying I approved of it."

HOW DO I CHOOSE A FUNERAL HOME?

Research Your Options

Narrow your choices down by asking family members or friends if they have used a funeral home they particularly liked and by visiting or phoning a few for more information. Then check your choices out by answering the following questions:

- What does the Better Business Bureau say about each one?
- When you Google their names, are there sites listing problems?
- Does the funeral home and staff hold the proper licenses?
- Do they provide price information over the phone?
- Do they provide a written list of all services?
- Is the funeral home intimidating?
- If you were to have a service at the funeral home, is it big enough to accommodate your needs?
- Is it convenient for family and friends?
- Is it the best bang for the buck, so to speak?
- Do they pressure you to choose the most expensive coffins on display?

HELP ME CHOOSE

Which of the following statements are true for you?
- I am very traditional.
- My family is very traditional.
- I like the idea of ashes to ashes, dust to dust.
- I like the idea of being buried in the earth.
- I like the idea of eternally resting above the ground.
- My family has a burial plot or mausoleum.

- I have resources to pay for a burial.
- I am most comfortable with a traditional cemetery.
- I would like to become a part of nature.
- I want room for other family members to be buried near me.
- I am comfortable with my money paying for perpetual care at traditional cemetery.
- I am comfortable with my money paying for conserving a tract of land.

Your answers will tell you which choice might be best for you.

CHAPTER 3

Into the Mystic:
Going Out in Flames Can Be a Good Thing

I read way too much Edgar Allen Poe in high school. It's not that I don't like his work, I do, but there is one story of his that I have never been able to get out of my mind. It's the "Cask of Amontillado," where Montresor buries Fortunato alive. Yeow! The thought of it gives me such a case of the creeps I can barely write the words. Yes, I have taphephobia, the fear of being buried alive. As Alice Cooper would say, "Welcome to My Nightmare." That's why I am so delighted about cremation and pleased that it is an option. Cremation can be practical, cost effective, and even good for the environment, but it's the stories of opening graves, years after burial, and finding claw marks on the inside of the coffins that have helped me make up my mind.

CREMATION

Cremation uses heat, vaporization, and flame to reduce the body to its basic elements. The body is placed into a container, which can be as simple as a cardboard box or as elaborate as a walnut coffin, then put into a retort, a specialized kind of oven. It is incinerated at a temperature of 760° to 1150°C (1400° to 2100°F), vaporizing and oxidizing soft tissue and drying the bones. This process usually takes about two hours. The remaining bone fragments are then pulverized in a cremulator. The end result, commonly called "cremains," looks like rough grains of sand with occasional bone fragments and generally weighs about three to nine pounds. The entire process can take as long as five hours.

Evidence of cremation has been found as early as the late Stone Age, with ornamental pottery urns having been discovered in western Russia. Ancient cremated remains have been found in fifty-six holes around the stones at Stonehenge. Cremation was the major way of disposing of bodies during the time of Homer in 800 B.C. and it was generally practiced in Roman times.

(Author's note: I have used the word "cremains" once appropriately. From here on out I'm going to use the word "ashes." The word "cremains" feels like it should be uttered by a lugubrious, hangdog, yellowing funeral director as he rubs his dry, scabrous hands together. So "ashes" it will be.)

Pros & Cons

This is the choice for people who quite simply do not want to be put in the ground and have dirt shoveled over top of them. Sing it, sister. You know where I stand. Others simply want to have the process over and done with rather than have their body decay in a grave. This is also a good choice if:

- You want a simple funeral process.

- You want to keep costs down. A straightforward cremation will be a fraction of the cost of a traditional burial.

- You want to help the environment by avoiding the use of a coffin, vault, and land. There is, however, growing evidence that the cremation process may have a significant impact on the environment by using non-renewal fossil fuel and emitting dioxins and other gasses.

- You want your remains placed outside of a cemetery. The EPA has rules about scattering ashes and you should research these rules, but in practice people put ashes everywhere. You might want your ashes scattered on the campus of your college—much easier than getting permission for your body to be buried beside the chemistry lab steps.

This is not a good choice if:

- Your religious beliefs prohibit cremation. Islam forbids cremation, Orthodox Judaism disapproves, but reformed Judaism supports the custom. The Greek Orthodox faith opposes cremation. Protestantism tends to allow it, while Roman Catholicism has become more lenient in its views.

- You and your family are quite traditional.

AN OLYMPIC TRIBUTE

Olympic volleyball player Misty May-Treanor's mom passed away in 2002 and didn't get to see her daughter compete in the 2004 and 2008 Olympics. After May-Treanor's two gold medal wins, Misty grabbed a small vial of her mother's ashes and scattered them on the sand of the volleyball courts.

IS CREMATION "GREENER"?

Greener than what, is the real question. Looking back at the pollution statistics listed in Chapter 2 for a traditional burial with embalming, casket, vault, and traditionally maintained cemetery, cremation certainly seems to win. But if you place cremation up against a completely green in-ground burial, you might decide to go with being buried in a nature preserve.

It does take a lot of energy to cremate a body. Some statistics state that the energy used is equivalent to driving 4,800 miles. There is a lively debate on the Internet about this. Some say the carbon emissions from a cremation equal that of cooking a hamburger—I know, this idea made me put down my cheeseburger, too. Others argue that while cremation's initial carbon footprint is high, it pales beside the carbon footprint created by maintaining the grounds for a traditional cemetery burial.

That said, it should be noted that crematoriums are beginning to use a higher grade of filters for their emissions. For more on this debate, you can visit this site: the Green Daily—**GreenDaily. com/2008/01/11/green-deathmatch-burial-vs-cremation**.

Costs

Cremation is one of the least expensive funeral practices if we are talking strictly about the costs of cremation versus burial costs. A general rule of thumb is that cremation can cost half of what a traditional burial costs. The amount of money you spend depends upon whether you want a simple cremation with friends or relatives spreading your ashes or you want a more traditional process that may include a viewing, a funeral home or church ceremony, and the burial of your ashes.

As with traditional in-ground burials, cremation prices are all over the map. There are dramatic differences between geographical areas and among funeral providers in any given area.

Direct Cremation Costs

Direct cremation is the least expensive option. This is cremation without embalming, a viewing, or funeral service, and usually it is combined with the selection of an inexpensive container. Some localities do not require the service of a funeral director for cremation. This means the crematorium will pick up the body and cremate it. Many states will let you obtain the death certificate and transportation permits so you can transport the body yourself. This will also keep costs down.

The following prices are from my informal survey of costs for direct cremation. These are low-end prices:

- Basic services for funeral director and staff: $99

- Crematory fee: $240

- Medical examiner fee (if required by law): $50
- Transfer vehicle: $85
- Transfer of remains: $125
- Simple container for cremation: $50
- A direct cremation package with a minimum container: $600.

The Funeral Consumers Alliance notes that if families care for their own dead and the body goes directly to the crematorium, the cost can be quite inexpensive, $300 or below.

Traditional Cremation Costs

The traditional route is more expensive than direct cremation but takes some of the burden off of loved ones. The funeral home or crematorium picks up the body, takes care of all of the paperwork, and presides over the entire process. The funeral home or crematorium will help you with such choices as embalming, viewing; church, funeral parlor, or home service; and so forth. The more options you choose to include, the more money you will spend.

The following prices generally reflect low-end pricing:

- Professional services of funeral director and staff: $1,495
- Crematory fee: $375
- Medical examiner fee (if required): $50
- Transfer of remains from funeral home to crematorium: $200
- Transfer of remains from place of death to funeral home: $275
- Simple container for cremation: $100
- Temporary container: $15
- A traditional funeral home cremation package: $995—$2,510.

Costs for the Pre-Cremation Container

As previously mentioned, you will be required to have a container for the body. It can be as simple as a corrugated cardboard box or as elaborate as a walnut casket. Most casket companies have a line of caskets built especially for the cremation process. The most inexpensive cremation casket starts around $350. Most funeral homes charge $100 or less for the cardboard container. More detailed information on caskets can be found in Chapter 4.

You can also "rent" a casket for a viewing, or the crematorium may provide a wooden shell that looks like a coffin and is removed after the service.

Crematoriums are required by law to have inexpensive containers available. You can also make your own container, provided it meets with the crematorium's requirements. See Chapter 4 for more information on making your own casket.

Costs for the Post-Cremation Container

After the cremation, the ashes will be returned to the family, along with a certificate of cremation and, if required by locality, a permit for disposition of human remains. The remains will be placed into either in a corrugated cardboard box with a plastic liner provided by the crematorium or in an urn you provide. If you are scattering your ashes, doing so from the crematorium's cardboard box might be just fine. If someone is keeping the ashes, you might want to spring for a fancy urn. Chapter 4 provides has more information about urns, including biodegradable urns and how to make your own urn.

Additional Fees

Additional fees you may run into include:

- Refrigeration—Not charged if the body will be embalmed: $25–$80 per day

- Topical disinfection—This is for the external cleansing of the body: $95–$295

- Embalming—This will be incurred only if you chose it: $380–$675

- Retrieval of ashes. An additional cost will be incurred if the ashes are mailed or otherwise delivered to another location. There should be no charge for picking them up.

- Placement of ashes. The final cremation cost with will be for the disposal of the ashes. You can pay for a traditional burial in a cemetery (the only way this differs from a traditional in-ground burial is that your ashes are being buried, not your body) or you can pay to place the ashes in a columbarium (a building or part of a building containing niches designed to hold and memorialize cremated remains). Your might hire a boat to scatter the ashes at sea or you may pay nothing but the cost of gas if you want to have your ashes scattered by family and friends.

STRAIGHT FROM THE SKY

A Chinese man, presumed to have been killed by lightning, was placed in a cremation chamber, only to have its doors fly off from the explosion of his body. A piece of metal found in the debris indicated that the man had actually been killed by a small undeployed weather rocket filled with silver iodide as it plunged to the earth. Want to read more? I thought so: "Body Explodes on Cremation": **AllWeirdNews.com/body-explodes-on-cremation**.

Service Choices

- Full traditional service. You can have a full, traditional funeral home or church service complete with embalming and viewing of the body. Later, the ashes may be buried in a cemetery, perhaps with a small private ceremony.

- Memorial service. You can have any kind of memorial service you wish, with or without the ashes present. It is obviously less costly if you have a simple cremation and a memorial service, perhaps at someone's home, where friends and family can gather and share memories.

- Limited service. You can have your body given a direct cremation with no service or just a small gathering at the crematorium before the body goes into the flames.

- No service. No one says there has to be a service of any kind.

How Do I Do It?

- Figure out exactly what you want. Then shop around. Remember, funeral homes and crematoriums are required to give you a price quote over the phone.

- Check to see if you are required to use the services of a funeral director. If not, and if you don't wish to use one, find out how to get the appropriate death certificate and transportation permits. Begin with a call to your local medical examiner's office.

- If you choose to use a funeral home and it does not have a crematorium, ask what the fee is for the home to work with a crematorium, including any accompanying costs and permit charges.

How Do I Choose a Crematorium?

Ask perspective crematoriums the following questions:

- Does the staff have voluntary certification by the Cremation Society of America?

- Do they have a code of ethics?

- What are their body tracking procedures so there's no chance of a mix-up?

- Can you tour the site?

- Can family or friends be present at the cremation?

- What is the lag time between body arrival and cremation?

- Can you see references?

Good To Know

- No federal law requires embalming. States rarely require it.

- No state or local law requires you to use a casket for cremation.

- Crematoriums or funeral homes cannot require you to buy an urn or casket from them.

- Most crematories require some type of stiff container that is burned with the body. The Federal Trade Commission rule of 1984 says that mortuaries must make available an unfinished wooden box or similar inexpensive cremation container. The rule also states that you may make or furnish your own suitable container.

- Remember, if you accompany the scattered ashes with wreaths or flowers, they should be biodegradable, especially if scattering them at sea.

- The Reverend Billy Graham wrote that he found nothing in the Bible that forbids cremation. **BillyGraham.org/MyAnswer_Article.asp?ArticleID=2402**

DISPOSAL OF ASHES

This is where it gets fun. Seriously. You can be shot into space, scattered to the four winds over the Grand Canyon, become a part of a coral reef, be made into a diamond ring, or even tossed into a hurricane, like WVEC-TV's Chief Meteorologist Jeff Lawson says he wants. You can also be sprinkled someplace you always wanted to visit but never did. I bet you can't go five steps down the Avenue des Champs-Elysées in Paris without kicking up someone's dust! Lets look at some options:

Traditional Burial of Ashes

You can have your ashes buried in a traditional cemetery in your own grave. Also, most cemeteries will let you bury ashes beside or above an existing coffin. In both cases, you will need a sturdy container or urn. Most cemeteries require a vault for the container. You will pay for opening and closing of the grave and attending expenses.

You can also bury ashes just about anywhere you want with the property owner's permission.

The types of containers for burying ashes range from fancy and expensive to homemade to eco-friendly biodegradable. We will discuss these in detail in Chapter 4.

Burial of Ashes at Sea

This is where an appropriate container holding your ashes is consigned to the deep. A funeral director is not required for the burial of cremated remains at sea. There are no federal or state laws that can stop you from performing this yourself, as long as you abide by local laws.

The Environmental Protection Agency states that "cremated remains [may] be buried in or on ocean waters …provided that such burial takes place at least three nautical miles from land." Notice has to be given to the EPA within 30 days of burial. Burial in inland waters is regulated according to the Clean Water Act. For inland waters burial, a permit is required from the appropriate state agency.

United States Navy Burial at Sea Program

The requirements for having ashes buried or scattered at sea by the United States Navy are the same as for full body burial at sea. These requirements are listed in Chapter 2. Forms and other information can be found at the United States Navy Mortuary Affairs Burial at Sea Program—**www.Navy.mil/navydata/questions/burial.html**. You can also call the United States Navy Mortuary Affairs office toll-free at 1-866-787-0081.

Not exactly the Yellow Submarine, but close. Consider making yourself a part of the ocean's ecosystem. The Neptune Memorial Reef is located a few miles off the Miami coast. *Photograph courtesy of Neptune Memorial Reef (NMReef.com)*

Memorial Reefs

Memorial reefs create new marine habitats for fish and other forms of sea life. You can be buried at sea in a living coral reef that has been constructed and pre-placed on the ocean floor. You can also be buried at sea in an ocean reef cast of concrete mixed with your ashes.

Placement in a Columbarium

Usually located in a cemetery mausoleum, a columbarium has niches to hold cremation urns. You will pay for the niche, the perpetual care, and the marker. Prices are all over the map, with some cemeteries charging up to $6,000 for a double niche and perpetual care. Then again, your place of worship may have a memorial columbarium for members who make a small donation.

On the Shelf

Ashes may be kept at home, of course. The major decision with this option would be the type of urn that will hold the ashes.

To the Four Winds

People have had their ashes scattered in as many different places as there are different places on Earth. You can have your ashes scattered a bit here, a bit there, a bit everywhere. First you need to know that cremated remains are sterile and pose no health hazard. They are also very white and don't blend in well with the dark soil in deep forests, so sprinkling them about may be necessary.

Scattering ashes is legal in most localities, but you need to check. For example, California has strict guidelines, one of which requires the family obtain a permit for disposition from the county health department. That said, trying to find what is permitted by searching state statutes can be difficult because most scattering regulations are controlled by local ordinance, with the exception of state and national parks. Do your best research, get permission from the landowners, and as Jiminy Cricket says, "Let your conscience be your guide."

You can be scattered by plane (beginning at $500), boat (anywhere from the cost of gas to a full crew and party at $5,000), fireworks ($4,000), cannon (depends on who owns the artillery), hot air balloon (begins around $300), or sent up in a biodegradable balloon ($400). I have a relative who loves to shoot his potato gun from my parents' deck overlooking the water. I have a feeling we'll be shooting him out of it one day. And no, I am not telling you where I live.

While you may decide to have your ashes scattered hither and yon, you might also want to have a place selected where friends and family can visit to grieve, celebrate, or share memories. Some people have a memorial marker placed beside the stream where they were scattered. Others may make a contribution to a national park, a school, or a hospital and have a marker placed there. It's something to think about. The different types of markers are discussed in Chapter 6.

Eco-Forests

These are green burial sites where ashes are placed beside memorial trees. A plaque is placed on the tree and your ashes nourish its growth. Prices for this can range from about $4,500 for an individual tree to $500 to join a neighborhood tree. The money goes toward maintaining the land.

National Parks

As the Talking Heads might say, "Take Me to the River." Most national parks will let you scatter ashes if you obtain permission and comply with a few commonsense rules, such as scattering remains out of public sight, away from water, and doing so over a large area so there is not a pile of ashes. While they will not let you leave a marker, some, like Yosemite National Park, have a memorial book in their chapels in which the deceased person's name can be recorded. You need to contact the individual park.

The Kitchen Sink

This is where creativity comes in. You can have your ashes made into almost anything. Here is a very short list. The related websites are provided at the end of this chapter. Get ready to smile.

Your ashes can be made into a picture frame ($150–$350), fountain ($400–$4,000), jewelry, a diamond ($3,500–$20,000), birdhouse ($300), artificial memorial ocean reef ($6,500–$25,000), lead in a pencil for your portrait to be drawn—this is actually true—($5,000–$8,000), potting soil for a memorial plant ($380), a memorial paperweight ($250), an hourglass ($240), Christmas ornaments, a Frisbee like "Steady" Ed Headrick, the father of the modern Frisbee, a teapot, a musical instrument, a bracelet ($275), a walking stick ($375), and on and on. Your ashes can also be incorporated into existing works of art. Anything and everything goes.

Beam Me Up, Scotty

Finally, you can have your ashes launched into space. This service seems to run anywhere from around $600 to have your ashes launched into space and returned, to around $10,000 to have your ashes placed on the surface of the moon, and then several thousand dollars more to have your ashes launched into deep space, never to return. Some companies will only transport a small amount of ashes, so it is good to have a plan for what to do with the extras.

It was good enough for James Doohan, chief engineer of the starship *Enterprise*, and Gene Roddenberry, *Star Trek* creator. It was also good enough for Timothy Leary, whose ashes were taken aloft in an American Pegasus rocket to orbit every 90 minutes for perhaps as many as 10 years. He should be coming down any time now. But then, who can say if he ever really will come down? If you have the money, why not?

A Note About Cremation Societies

Not every business calling itself a "society" is a nonprofit. There is no restriction on the use of the term, so some consumers might believe that a certain cremation society is run like the nonprofit memorial societies, only to get a big surprise after they join. If you are considering joining such a group, do your research and be sure to read the fine print.

Punk Rock Upset

Sid Vicious of the Sex Pistols wanted his ashes to be put with his late soul mate Nancy Spungen. Some believe that his ashes were indeed scattered over Spungen's Pennsylvania grave in the dead of night by his mother. But according to the U.K. newspaper *The Guardian*, his mother accidentally spilled the urn's contents and Sid's ashes were unceremoniously scattered in Heathrow Airport's arrivals lounge. The Internet abounds with differing versions of this entertaining story.

THE NEWEST THING

Alkaline hydrolysis, or water resolution, is being touted as the next best thing to cremation. This process uses heated water, pressure, and alkalinity to accelerate the natural decomposition process (in as little as 30 minutes), leaving a liquid that can be dried into a form resembling ashes.
BioSafeEngineering.com/waterresolution/about.html

THE SECOND NEWEST THING

Developed by Susan Wiigh-Masak of Promessa Organic, a new process freezes the body to minus 18 Celsius and submerges it in liquid nitrogen. The result is an extremely brittle corpse that is then vibrated until it turns into an organic powder. Fascinating. Check this web site for more details: **Promessa.se/sagardettill_en.asp**.

Diamonds can indeed be a best friend if you turn yourself or a loved one's remains into a certified, high-quality piece of jewelry. *Photograph courtesy of LifeGem (LifeGem.com)*

ON THE WEB

- Angels Flight—Your ashes sent up in fireworks. Just like Hunter Thompson: **Angels-Flight.net**.

- Art from Ashes—Ashes are made into memorial glass objects: **ArtFromAshes.com**.

- Celestis—Your ashes can orbit the earth, land on the moon's surface or delve into deep space. Gene Roddenberry's choice. **MemorialSpaceflights.com**

- Creative Cremains—Where artists turn ashes into single pieces of art or incorporate ashes into existing pieces of art: **Creative Cremains.com/home.html**.

- Cremation.com—Search for a cremation provider in your locality: **Cremation.com**.

- Cremation.org—Site for finding a low-cost cremation society or cremation service provider in your area. There is a fee for joining these societies and you should shop with great care. **Cremation.org**

- Cremation Solutions—Have your ashes made into soil to grow a memorial plant: **CremationSolutions.com/Floramorial-living-cremation-memorial-c45.html**.

- EcoEternity Forest—An alternative green burial site where ashes are placed beside memorial trees: **EcoEternity.com**.

- EPA—Site for EPA regulations regarding sea burial: **EPA.gov/region4/water/oceans/burial.htm**.

- Eternal Reefs—An underwater, environmentally safe, cast-concrete ball that is used to create new marine habitats for fish and other forms of sea life: **EternalReefs.com**.

- Great Burial Reef—Featuring sea burial in a living coral reef: **GreatBurialReef.com**.

- How to Build a Potato Gun—Enough said: **HubPages.com/hub/how_to_build_a_potato_gun.**

- The Environmental eZine—A discussion of the environmental impact of green burial, traditional interment, and cremation: **lilith-ezine.com/articles/environmental/Green-Burials.html.**

- National Park Service—Site for contacting the national parks about scattering ashes: **NPS.gov.**

- Over The Rainbow—A selection of memorial objects made from cremated ashes. Products include sun catchers, pendants, bracelets, rings, and other great things: **OTRMemorials.com.**

- WalesOnline—An article about a son who turns his dad's ashes into a teapot: **WalesOnline.co.uk/news/wales-news/2008/07/06/welshman-turns-dad-s-ashes-into-tea-pot-91466-21269042.**

HELP ME CHOOSE

Which of the following statements are true for you?

- I want a simple funeral process.

- I want to keep costs down.

- My religious beliefs support cremation.

- I have environmental concerns with a full burial.

- I would like my remains placed somewhere outside of a cemetery.

- My family would condone this nontraditional type of process.

- My family needs a traditional ritual.

Your answers will tell you which choice might be best for you.

Chapter 4

Thinking Inside the Box

My family owns a great coffin. We use it every Halloween to scare the living bejeebers out of trick-or-treaters. My father makes a grand "Digger O'Dell" standing beside it, dressed in a tattered suit and holding a shovel. While our coffin may not meet the exact requirements for burial in a traditional memorial park, it sure serves its intended purpose. And that's what this chapter is all about, having the right container to hold our mortal remains—Oh man, now *I'm* starting to sound like Digger O'Dell.

This chapter will explore choices for coffins and urns from traditional to green to self-made. The chapter is divided into two sections; the first is about coffins for full body burial, and the second talks about coffins for cremation and urns for the ashes. This chapter will help you make the important decision as to what fits your personal needs. Because after all, you don't want to be like Larry LaPrise, the man who wrote "The Hokey Pokey," do you? Larry died peacefully at age 93. When they put him in his coffin they put his left leg in. And that's when the trouble started.

Full Body Burial

I've said it before and I'll say it again: There is no state or federal law requiring that a body be buried in a casket. However, cemeteries may demand it. Traditional cemeteries usually demand that the coffin be protected by a vault as well.

There is no state or federal law requiring you to purchase a coffin from a funeral director. There are some states, such as Virginia, Louisiana, and Oklahoma, that allow only funeral directors to *sell* coffins. You can get around this by making one yourself, ordering one by mail or Internet, or even buying one from some of the big membership stores. Costco sells traditional coffins, starting at $924.99. Walmart also sells caskets, starting at $895, with free shipping to the store for pickup. Keep in mind that you can always rent a casket for a viewing or ceremony.

The good news here is that there are a million (well, almost) different caskets available if you decide to go the traditional route. You can always call the Batesville Casket Company in Indiana and order a custom-made, hand-polished casket, just like the one they made for Michael Jackson. With its shining gold and bronze exterior and crushed-velvet interior, it will only run you about $25,000. And there are a million-and-one choices for a nontraditional casket if you decide to get creative. Think of caskets shaped like tennis shoes, pianos, sailboats, you name it. Very fun. Lets get started.

FULL BODY BURIAL—TRADITIONAL CASKETS

A traditional coffin is defined as a box or case in which the body of a dead person is placed for burial. Coffins are also called caskets.

Wood Caskets

- Wood caskets can be made of any type of wood, including pine, oak, maple, birch, cherry, mahogany, and walnut. The wood can be veneer or mixed.

- The most commonly used wood is poplar, because it can be stained to look like almost any other type of wood.

- Most wood caskets are not constructed with a gasket and cannot be sealed upon closing. (A gasket is a rubber seal used to close the coffin for the last time.)

- Most wood caskets latch rather than lock.

Metal Caskets

- Metals used for caskets include stainless steel, copper, sheet bronze, and even cast bronze.

- Steel caskets come in three different gauges, or degrees, of thickness. Stainless steel comes in two different grades: basic and premium.

- Copper and bronze caskets are the most durable since they are naturally non-rusting materials.

- And then there is the choice of being buried in a 14-carat-gold plated casket, like the Godfather of Soul, James Brown.

- Most metal caskets are constructed with a gasket at the openings so that they can be sealed upon closing.

- Most metal caskets are lockable from the outside.

Caskets for Burial at Sea

- Coffins used for sea burials have specific requirements designed to allow quick descent.

- You can use a weighted body bag, sailcloth, or a specially converted coffin.

- Your maritime funeral provider will have the details.

Pros & Cons

- A traditional casket can be very expensive.

- There is a wide variety of traditional coffins to choose from.

- Selecting a traditional coffin is often easiest.

- You cannot be buried in a green burial ground if you have a traditional casket.

Costs

The average price for a casket today is approximately $2,000. A simple pine casket usually runs around $300. The most expensive casket I've been able to find tops out at $48,000. As you can see, casket choice is truly a matter of personal taste.

Wood caskets, listed here from the least expensive to most expensive, are made from pine, oak, maple, birch, cherry, mahogany, and walnut. A casket made with an outer veneer of an expensive type of wood looks pretty much the same as one crafted completely from expensive solid wood, but usually costs a lot less.

Steel caskets vary in price according to the thickness of the steel and they are usually the most affordable caskets available. Stainless steel caskets are usually in the mid-price range of all the caskets. Bronze and copper are the most expensive, and these can cost on the far side of $10,000. Cast bronze is the most expensive of all.

How Do I Do It?

Research coffins well before you need one. Compare appearance, features, and prices just like you would for any other purchase. The Internet provides, as always, a wealth of information, and using the Internet to comparison shop is often easier and less intimidating than dealing with retailers. Once you have gotten some general information off the Internet, you can proceed to contacting local suppliers.

Also, check with your local Funeral Consumers Alliance, which can supply you with the names of reputable dealers.

Good to Know

- The Federal Trade Commission's "Funeral Rule" states that funeral homes must show you a list of all the funeral caskets they sell, complete with prices and descriptions, before actually showing you their funeral caskets.

- The FTC also states that a funeral home may not refuse to use a casket purchased elsewhere.

- Funeral homes are also forbidden to charge a handling fee if you order a casket on your own; this includes "inspection" fees.

- The funeral home should not require the family to be present to accept the casket.

RING IN THE COFFIN

They say that everything eventually dies. So, if your marriage does, you can give it a final resting place with The Wedding Ring Coffin. This is a perfect gift to help bring closure or to send to your ex in the mail. Why didn't I think of that? **WeddingRingCoffin.com**

On the Web

- Caskets by Design—For larger folks. Reasonably priced. **CasketsByDesign.com**

- Funerals On-Line—Lots of good information, including a U.S. Funeral Guide & Comprehensive Funeral Homes Directory. **US-Funerals.com/caskets.html**

- The Casket Place—Will send you information about buying caskets online. **TheCasketPlace.com/freeeguide.htm**

FULL BODY BURIAL—NONTRADITIONAL CASKETS

Nontraditional coffins are becoming more and more prevalent. Many people use them as a final statement of what they stood for while before shuffling off this mortal coil. Here are some ideas to get you started:

- You can have a traditional casket decorated with art. Grand Departures has caskets decorated for hunters, firemen, bikers, and people of other ilks, beginning at $3,999. **GrandDepartures.com/subcategory_show.cfm?id=28**

- You can have your ancestry reflected at Two Feathers Coffins and Caskets. Their coffins are handmade by native craftsman, using birch, spruce, maple, and pine. Native artists decorate the coffins. Prices begin at $999. **TwoFeathersCoffins.com**

- You can choose to have your coffin made by the Trappist monks of New Melleray Abbey, whose casket-making is an extension of their sacred work. Simple coffins start at about $975. **TrappistCaskets.com**

Pros & Cons

- A nontraditional casket may be the way to go if you do indeed want to make a final statement.

- A nontraditional casket can provide levity in a sad situation.

- It can give your going away party a bit of sass.

- If you are planning to be buried in a traditional cemetery, the size and shape of your nontraditional coffin might dictate a custom-made vault and this could run into quite a bit of money.

- Most nontraditional coffins are made of products that are not allowed into a green burial ground.

- Not all traditional burial sites will accommodate nontraditional coffins.

Costs

A nontraditional casket often costs more because of the extra labor that goes into its design and construction. But for the guy who wants to be buried in a beer bottle-shaped coffin, perhaps the expense is worth it.

How Do I Do It?

Go on the Internet and visit some of the places I've listed below. Or just Google "unusual coffins." I guarantee you can spend days surfing the Web on this subject.

On the Web

- Art Caskets—Casket exteriors are decorated with full-color photographs, artwork, and imagery that reflect the life of the deceased. **ArtCaskets.com**

- Crazy Coffins—For more ideas, such as having a coffin shaped like an egg, a tennis racquet, a skateboard, a duffel bag, a guitar, or a wine cork. **www.CrazyCoffins.co.uk**

Can't let go of your cell phone? Then go to your final resting place in a Nokia. These hand-sculpted wooden coffins are made by the famous GA coffin carpenters in Accra, Ghana, and can be ordered online. *Photograph courtesy of eShopAfrica.com*

Full Body Burial—Green Caskets

Green caskets are made from fully biodegradable products such as wood, wicker, willow, bamboo, sea grass, water hyacinth, banana leaves, corn skin, and paper. Eco-friendly or biodegradable caskets are free from varnish, plastic, metal, toxic glue, oil, or animal products. Some green coffins use only wood that comes from sustainable forests. Usually, rope handles are provided. Green caskets can help reduce your "carbon footprint," which is the sum of all of CO_2 (carbon dioxide) emissions produced by your activities in a given time frame.

Most manufacturers of green caskets are also concerned about using fair trade wood, the carbon footprint for shipping, the amount of energy they use in production, and other ecological matters. For example, EcoCoffins, USA, offers woven bamboo coffins made from bamboo that pandas will not eat, and that is grown and cut under license from the Chinese government.

Pros & Cons

- Green coffins help the environment, especially if you buy from a manufacturer who is concerned with its company's carbon footprint.

- If anyone needs forensic evidence about you or your death down the road, most of it would be destroyed by the accelerated decomposition that attends being buried in a biodegradable coffin.

- A green coffin is considered by most to be ideal for orthodox Jewish burial.

- Green coffins can usually be buried in any type of cemetery, from green to traditional.

- Traditional cemeteries usually demand a burial vault covering. This would seem to defeat the purpose of trying to be environmentally friendly. I'm just saying....

Costs

As with traditional caskets, the price varies from several hundred dollars to as high as you want to go. It simply depends on your budget. Some 2009 Internet prices were:

- Caskets By Design—Eco-friendly cedar casket on sale for $949, plus shipping. **CasketsByDesign.com/Wood_Caskets.html**

- Environmental Caskets—Made from certified sustainably harvested wood: $2,795, with next day free delivery. **EnvironmentalCaskets.com**

- Kent Caskets—This green casket lists for $420, including shipping. **KentCasket.com**

How Do I Do It?

This is easy. Simply go to the websites listed below and begin your research. You should have already picked out how you want to be buried and where. Now, let those choices guide you to the correct coffin.

Good to Know

- The green burial movement is gaining momentum and the Internet abounds with good, solid information.

- Green coffins can vary in price as much as $1,000 between different suppliers, so shopping online or by phone is a must.

- Green caskets do not have to look goofy. Well, some people worry about this type of thing. Apollo caskets are very cool. They are originally hand-carved in clay, then cast in a "green" biopolymer made from corn. This material acts like a hardwood in the ground. These caskets can also be cremated, producing less pollution than other caskets. **ApolloCasket.com**

Reduce your carbon footprint by choosing the naturally biodegradable Eco-pod. The earth will thank you. *Photograph courtesy of ARKA Ecopod Limited (EcoPod.co.uk)*

On the Web

- Eco Coffins—All natural coffins: **EcoCoffins.com.**

- Green Casket Company—Their caskets and casket kits are made in Asheville, North Carolina, using all local, organic products: **GreenCasket.net.**

- Ecoffins USA—A site for coffins made from bamboo, banana, and so forth. **EcoffinsUsa.com**

THE ETERNAL POLE DANCE

If you are the practical sort, you might want to visit **Casket-Furniture.com**, where a couch, shelf, or end table can be transformed into a high-quality casket when you die. They actually have a stripper-stage casket with pole included. It might help you squeeze through the pearly gates—or not. CasketFurniture.com/casket_furniture.php

---

FULL BODY BURIAL—HOMEMADE CASKETS

Homemade caskets are exactly that. Whether you make them from wood harvested on your own land or buy a kit on the Internet, a homemade casket can save you money and help you prepare mentally for your upcoming event. It can celebrate your life and remind people of exactly what made you so doggone special. Here's an idea—why not have a casket-building party for friends and family? It would be a nice coming-together event and perhaps help with the premourning process. Just be sure to limit the beer!

Pros & Cons

- A handmade casket is a good idea if you want to save money or participate in the process that will close your life's final chapter.

- It is a nice choice if you want a green or home burial.

- Not everyone is a carpenter, so when ordering a kit you will want to make sure that you can follow the plans and have the proper tools.

Costs

Casket-making kits are surprisingly inexpensive. Here are some prices as of 2009:

- Bert & Bud's Vintage Coffins sells a coffin kit for a pine or poplar wedge-shaped coffin for $795. The coffin kit comes with the unfinished box and lid, sanded to a beautiful finish. Handles and clear-coat finish can be added at additional cost. The coffin kit can also be purchased fully assembled at no additional cost, although shipping charges will be slightly higher. **VintageCoffins.com**

- Casket Express had its casket kit on sale for $599.97, marked down from $1,100. **CasketXpress.com/item/1195703077.html**

- Casket Furniture and Casket Kits sell kits, starting at $895 for a simple pine coffin kit: **CasketFurniture.com**.

- MHP Casket Kits start around $795. **MHP-CasketKits.com**

- Sweet Earth Casket and Cradle Shop sells casket kits for $800. **SweetEarthCaskets.com/site.php**

How Do I Do It?

You should start by researching on the Internet. Several excellent sites are listed below. Contact your local Funeral Alliance for local statutes. Also be sure to find out the requirements for your cemetery.

Good to Know

- There are no specific requirements regarding caskets in any state.

- If you are using a traditional cemetery, be sure that the coffin fits the size requirements for the underground vault.

- An average casket is 6'4" long, 24" wide, and about 30" deep.

- You can be buried in a homemade casket in just about any cemetery.

- Green burial sites will want reassurance that the construction materials are biodegradable and ecologically friendly.

- Traditional cemeteries will have their own requirements, including the seemingly ubiquitous burial vault, so it is best to check first before making a casket.

- Burial at sea will require you to check with a local maritime funeral provider about special marine coffin requirements.

On the Web

- Last Things: Alternatives at the End of Life—How to make a quick coffin. **LastThings.net/how-to.html**

- Mother Earth News—This article tells you what you need to know to create simple, beautiful, and inexpensive wooden caskets. **MotherEarthNews.com/Green-Homes/2003-04-01/Homemade-Caskets.aspx**

- The North House Folk School in Grand Marais, Minnesota— They offers a build-your-own-casket workshop called "Bury

Yourself In Your Work." The three-day session runs $255 for tuition and $470 for materials. **NorthHouse.org**

- Rockler Woodworking and Hardware—wood casket plans. **Rockler.com/CategoryView.cfm?Cat_ID=140&filter=casket**

- Teach Me! Show Me!—How to build a coffin. **TeachMeShowMe.com/build-a-coffin.php**

CREMATION COFFINS AND URNS

For cremation, you will need a casket or container to hold the body before and during cremation and a container for the ashes afterwards. Let's start by noting that according to the FTC's Funeral Rule, no state or local law requires you to use a casket for cremation. That said, there are three basic types of pre-cremation containers you can use: traditional coffins, crematorium-provided containers, and alternative containers.

PRE-CREMATION TRADITIONAL COFFINS

A traditional cremation coffin is the same as a traditional coffin used for burial, with the exception that it meets cremation requirements. Cremation caskets are generally made entirely of wood or wood by-products, and the use of metal is kept to a minimum.

Pros & Cons

- Buying a coffin that is going to go up in ashes is not a good idea if you are trying to save money.

Costs

The cost of a traditional coffin for cremation is frequently less expensive than an in-ground burial casket, so it depends on how much you are willing to spend. The coffin can be as simple or elaborate as you desire. You can purchase cremation coffins yourself or obtain one through a funeral home.

How Do I Do It?

You purchase your casket as noted above in the "Full Body Burial" section, but make sure it is a casket designed for cremation.

Good to Know

- If you are just going to use the casket for a service or viewing, it is a good idea to rent one. Funeral homes often provide this service.

- Usually, people use a traditional casket for cremation if they are having a formal service with the casket present for a viewing.

On the Web

- The Funeral Casket Society—This company sells cremation caskets, starting at $795. **CasketSite.com/type/cremation.htm**

- ABC Caskets Factory—They sell cremation caskets, starting at $356. **ABetterCasket.com**

PRE-CREMATION CREMATORIUM-PROVIDED CONTAINERS

The Federal Trade Commission rules of 1984 state that mortuaries must make available an unfinished wooden box or similar inexpensive container for cremations. Most of these are heavy, corrugated cardboard boxes.

Pros and Cons

- This is a good idea if you are having a direct cremation.

- These are excellent for limiting costs.

- These are not a good choice if you want to have a formal service, unless you rent a "show casket."

Costs

A container provided by the crematorium will usually run any-where from $75 to $150. Costs vary, depending on your geographic location and the service provider.

PRE-CREMATION COFFINS—ALTERNATIVE, HANDMADE, GREEN

The Federal Trade Commission rules of 1984 state that you may make or furnish your own suitable container. Specific information on homemade and green coffins can be found in the previous section. Whatever you choose, make sure it is acceptable for cremation use. You can purchase a cardboard coffin on the Internet.

Pros and Cons

- Good for those who want to involve their family and friends with the making of a homemade coffin.

- Also good for those who want to help the environment by choosing a green coffin.

- Excellent for those who want to save money with an alternative choice.

On the Web

- Memorials.com—This site sells Dignified Cremation Caskets constructed of heavy-test corrugated cardboard. They are easy to assemble. Price: $197.95
  Memorials.com/Caskets/Dignified-Cremation-Caskets.php

- The Natural Burial Company—This site offers environmentally friendly burial products and services.
  NaturalBurialCompany.com

> **DRIVE-IN BURIAL**
>
> Sandra Ilene West, a Texas millionaire oil heiress, requested and was buried in her lace nightgown, sitting at a comfortable slant behind the wheel of her powder-blue 1964 Ferrari 250GT at the Alamo Masonic Lodge Cemetery in San Antonio, Texas, in 1977. West and her Ferrari were buried in a large box that was covered with two truckloads of cement to discourage vandals.

POST-CREMATION CONTAINERS—URNS

The container that holds your ashes can reflect your hobbies and interests. It can be decorative or practical or both. The first thing to consider is how the container will be used. Will it be used for display, kept in the back of the closet, used to scatter the ashes, dropped into the sea, buried, or made into several small containers to hand out to different members of the family? There are lots of ideas here. Let's take a further look.

TRADITIONAL URNS

This is what you see sitting on mantles and in display cases. These types of urns are purchased from the crematorium or other funeral products providers. They can also be purchased online.

Pros & Cons

- Traditional urns are good for display or used as part of a formal memorial service.

- The expense isn't outrageous.

Costs

Once again, the price range is all over the map. You can pay as little as $50 or you can go completely nuts and the price will climb accordingly. It's all a matter of what you want. An informal survey of urn prices from funeral homes showed a range from $15 to $3,000.

If you decide that your urn will be buried in a traditional cemetery, you will usually need a vault for the urn. At Memorial Urns, vaults start at $49.99. **Memorial-Urns.com/urn_vault.html**

How Do I Do It?

Your funeral home or crematorium will provide you with a selection of urns. You may also look on the Internet to find other providers, a larger range of choices, and better prices. Your nearby Dollar Tree store might even have something that can be used!

Good to Know

- Traditional urns are used with formal services.

- They can also be placed in a columbarium, buried, or displayed.

- Traditional urns are not allowed in burials at sea and green cemeteries because of the materials from which they are made.

- According to the FTC's "Funeral Rule," crematoriums and funeral homes cannot require you to buy an urn from them.

- The FTC's "Funeral Rule" requires that a funeral provider who offers cremations must make alternative containers available.

- Cremation urns are sized by the cubic inch. One pound of body weight will yield roughly one cubic inch of ashes.

On the Web

- Overstock—This site has plenty of burial urns, ranging from a $99.99 natural-earth cultured marble urn to a $229.99 walnut burl with birch inlay urn. **OverStock.com**

- Memorial Urns and Tributes—A site with a huge selection of urns. **Memorial-Urns.com**

Nontraditional Urns

An urn that reflects your tastes and defines how you want to be remembered may be more to your liking. Urns are now made in almost any shape and size and from almost any material you can imagine. Urns are now available that use state-of-the-art 3D imaging and photographs to create a bust-type urn in the shape of the deceased. No matter what you want, you will probably be able to find it.

Nontraditional urns include:

- Companion urn—An urn that can accommodate two adults or one large adult.

- Keepsake urn—A keepsake urn is usually a tiny (one to two cubic inches) urn-shaped container or a glass pendant that holds a small portion of ashes. These can be handed out to family and friends.

- Scattering urn—There are now urns used specifically for scattering of ashes. Some folks don't want to go with the plain cardboard box provided by the crematorium.

- Specialty urn—Urns shaped as cowboy boots, motor speedways, lighthouses, wildlife, or golf clubs. Some even have digital photo frame urns. You name it.

Costs

A nontraditional urn can cost as much as you are willing to pay. A cast bronze, special-made urn will run you thousands of dollars, while a cute urn shaped like a butterfly, cast in less costly material, can run about $40. Small keepsake urns and glass pendant necklace keepsake urns also run about $40. Hourglass urns that use your ashes start at $250.

How Do I Do It?

The best thing is to go on the Internet and do your research, starting with the web sites listed below.

Good to Know

- These urns can be used with any type of service.

- These urns can be displayed in the home, they can be placed in a columbarium, or they can be buried.

- They may not be allowed in burials at sea and in green cemeteries (depending on the materials from which they are made).

- You can find urns on sale and you can find urns at discount prices.

- If you Google "YOURWORD urns" where "YOURWORD" describes your special interest or hobby, you will probably find just what you are looking for.

On the Web

- Elegant Urns—A selection of unusual urns. **ElegantUrns.com**

- In the Light Urns—A selection of keepsake urns. **InTheLightUrns.com**

- Overstock—A selection of keepsake urns. **OverStock.com/Health-Beauty/Keepsakes/3110/cat.html**

- Shine On Brightly—Artistic urns of all shapes and sizes. **ShineOnBrightly.com**

- Traditional Scattering Urns—A selection of urns used specifically for scattering ashes. **UrnWholesaler.com/type/scattering.htm**

- Digital Photo Frame Urn by Memory Vault—This urn can hold up to 1,000 photos, and it has the capability to play audio and video files. It can also hold multiple loved ones. **MemoryVaultOnline.com/photo.html**

- Cremation Solutions—Provides custom-made personalized cremation urns using state-of-the-art 3D imaging and photographs to create an urn in the image of a loved one. **CremationSolutions.com/Personal-Urns-c109.html**

GREEN URNS

Green urns are made from natural substances and are biodegradable. They are non-toxic, environmentally safe, and dissolve completely in water.

Pros and Cons

- If you want to be environmentally friendly, this is the way to go.
- You might want to note that the greens urns that are buried degrade rapidly. Some might be uncomfortable with this.

Costs

Some green urns start at $75, if found on sale. Others include a biodegradable bag and start at $39. You can certainly go much higher if you want some bells and whistles.

How Do I Do It?

Again, get on the Internet. Shop for bargains. Compare rates and remember to include shipping costs in your estimates.

Good to Know

- Green urns can be used for scattering, burial in both a conventional or green cemetery, and burial at sea.
- Before burying an urn, be sure to check your cemetery's requirements. If the urn is to be buried in a traditional cemetery, you will probably need to buy a vault.
- Finding a green urn is very easy on the Internet, since the green burial movement is becoming increasingly popular.
- A majority of the green sites are based in the United Kingdom, since they are far ahead of the U.S. regarding green burial. So be sure to order from a U.S. (and not U.K.) site.

On the Web

- EverLife Memorials—Beautiful and affordable biodegradable urns. **EverLifeMemorials.com/v/urns/biodegradable-urns.htm**
- Urn Garden—Biodegradable-green burial urns. **urngarden.com/Cremation_Urns-Biodegradable_Cremation_Urns/c1_9/index.html**

HOMEMADE URNS

You can make your own urn. Put one together from pieces of wood, carve one, make one in a pottery class, or make a mold and pour yourself a cement urn. Just about anything goes.

Pros and Cons

- If used in a green burial, the urn must meet environmental standards.
- If used in a traditional burial, the urn must meet cemetery requirements.
- Making your own urn is good if you want to involve your family and friends.
- It can be uncomfortable for family and friends to assist, or they may disapprove of something "homemade." Whatever would Great Aunt Ethel think?

Good to Know

Even though it is hard to find urn-making plans on the Internet, there are plenty of sites that describe how to make pet urns. Well, why not? Just be sure to make your own urn bigger than Fluffy's.

On the Web

- MHP Urns—Plans for affordable urns. **MHP-Urns.com/urn_plans.php**
- Wood Pet Urns—Plans for making pet urns. **WoodPetUrns.com**

- Woodworking Corner—Animal urns.
  WoodWorkingCorner.com/cremationbox.php

Traveling with Cremated Remains

Having to travel with cremated remains happens more often than you would imagine. Here are some things to note:

- Passengers are allowed to carry a crematory container as part of their carry-on luggage, but the container must pass through the X-ray machine.

- Carrying remains through scanners can be difficult if the urn or container is made of metal, ceramic, or certain types of stone. Your best option is to use a temporary or permanent crematory container made of a lighter-weight material, such as wood or plastic, that can be successfully x-rayed.

- Documentation from the funeral home is not sufficient to bypass screening.

- A screener will never open the container, even if the passenger requests this be done.

- Some airlines do not allow cremated remains as checked baggage.

- Here is the Transportation Security Administration website: **www.TSA.gov/travelers/airtravel/specialneeds/ editorial_1296.shtm**.

Help Me Choose

Which of the following statements are true for you?

- I am very traditional and want to be buried in a traditional cemetery.

- I am not traditional.

- I want to add some sass to my final going-away.

- I want to make a statement with my coffin/urn.

- I have money set aside for a coffin/urn.

- I would like to become a part of nature—green is me.

- I like the idea of everyone pitching in and building my coffin or urn.

- I think the less expensive the pre-cremation container the better.

- I want a formal display of my ashes.

- I'm going to be scattered and I don't care about the urn.

Your answers will tell you which choice might be best for you.

CHAPTER 5

It's My Party ...

Whispering behind their hands, the ladies walked through the room, their black dresses swishing against their legs. One of them paused for a moment and, bending down, switched off the television. I opened my mouth to protest and a white-gloved hand closed on my shoulder, stopped my words, and gently pulled me up from my spot on the sofa. Aunt Sudie needed to lie down. She needed it to be quiet. The heat and emotion of the day were proving too much for her to bear.

Gravel crunched in the driveway and there was a stir in the house. Women gathered up paper fans and the men unwillingly shrugged into their suit coats. The children stayed behind, watching as dust followed the cars out onto the road. The adults were going somewhere private, to a place where they cried, a place they wouldn't talk about, a place that made Aunt Sudie pass out on the sofa before she even got there. A funeral.

Dark, grim, foreboding, spoken about only in whispers, these are my childhood memories of funerals. The thought of going to one of these scared me half to death. I didn't want to wind up on the sofa like poor Aunt Sudie.

Fast-forward some thirty odd years. I'm sitting in Kathie's house, sucking down my third gin and tonic, roaring with laughter over stories about my friend whom we had just buried. Rock-n-roll is blasting through the speakers, Randy is getting ready to read his tribute to Robert, champagne is being poured for the toast, and if there is any passing out on the sofa, it sure won't be done by Aunt Sudie.

WHY A CELEBRATION IS IMPORTANT

Whether it's drinking margaritas at someone's home or singing hymns at a High Episcopal service, you are participating in a celebration of a person's life, a ritual that is not only proper, it is necessary. Don't look at me that way. A celebration *is too* necessary and you are going to use this chapter to plan your own so your family and friends won't go berserk trying to figure out what you would have wanted.

Think about it for a moment. Here is your final (pun intended) chance to get in the last word. You can tell everyone how much they meant to you, you can ask them to please donate to your favorite cause, you can let everyone and God know that you harbored a secret love for your cousin, you can even come out of the closet posthumously. What ever would Aunt Sudie say? Personally, I intend to let everyone know that, despite my parents' threats to cut off my tuition and their subsequent forty years of bragging that I caved in to their demands, I really *did* march on Washington D.C. to protest the Vietnam War.

See? That's not so bad. Planning can be a good thing. You can do this and you should. You do it not only to leave a game plan for those left behind holding the bag, but for closure. And closure is very important. A service can help your friends and family reach that final, important stage of acceptance where they can get on with their lives. What? Did you want them to hang around forever mourning you? People only do that in Shakespeare. Let's get going and figure out what you want for your final hurrah.

The Celebration

The celebration ceremony you will have depends on several things:

- The type of service you want: funeral, memorial, committal, or alternative
- The format of the service: religious, nonreligious, family gathering, private
- The disposition of your body in the manner you have chosen: body bequeathing, direct disposition, self-service, or traditional care by a funeral home
- The type of cemetery you have chosen: national, public, nonprofit, religious, commercial, green, or family
- The type of burial you have chosen in Chapters 2 or 3: full body, cremation, in-ground, green, at sea, at home, alternative, scattering of ashes
- Practical considerations such as location
- Religious considerations
- Financial circumstances
- How you want to be remembered.

The choices you have made using the information in previous chapters will indicate what type of celebration might be appropriate. You might read this chapter, decide on just the right celebration, and have to go back and change some aspects of your other choices. That's why pencils were invented. This can be mix-and-match, so let's get started figuring it out.

TYPE OF SERVICE

The four basic types of services are funeral, memorial, committal, and alternative. Your service should reflect how you see yourself and how you want to be remembered. If you are traditional in style and form, then by all means, plan the traditional funeral. If you have been a bit of a rebel, then a memorial service held in your favorite bar before opening time (after closing time?) might be just the thing. If you are a nature lover and an environmentalist, then a service out in the woods with people being asked to donate money to one of your causes might be fine. You might be like Paul Newman, who said, "The trick to living is to slip on and off the planet with the least fuss you can muster." A small service would suit. Me? I'm choosing champagne on the beach.

TRADITIONAL FUNERAL SERVICE

A traditional service is the full-tilt-boogie ceremony, the time-honored event you always see in the movies, and the type we remember from our childhoods. Characteristics of a traditional funeral:

- There is a formal viewing and/or visitation in the funeral home a day or two before the service.

- This type of ceremony is usually held with either a standard cemetery burial or cremation.

- The service itself is usually lengthy and presided over by clergy.

- The body is present in a casket or the cremation urn is present.

- There are one or two eulogies and a formal reading or two.

- The casket or urn is transported to the cemetery for burial, or the casket is transported to the crematorium after the service.

- If you are a member of a church or have another religious affiliation, the type of ceremony may be dictated by this affiliation.

Location of Service

- You can choose anyplace that will suit the logistics. Usually the ceremony is held in a church or funeral home.

- If you use a funeral director, he will likely want a say about the arrangements.

Type of Cemetery

- Burial is usually in a traditional cemetery.

Pros & Cons

- If you or your loved ones enjoy long-established rituals, this type of service is the way to go.

- This is an always acceptable choice that will offend the fewest people.

- Often provides closure for your loved ones.

- This can be a very expensive choice to make.

Costs

Chapter 2 lists the costs associated with a full body, in-ground burial and traditional funeral service. The Cremation Association of North America and the National Funeral Directors Association project that the average cost of an adult funeral will soon be $7,323. The national median cost for calendar year 2006 was $6,195. And that does not include costs for the plot, marker, flowers, or obituary. This amounts to about 13 percent of the median American family's annual income.

Good to Know

- Even if the service is going to be traditional, you can add personal touches that make it speak of how you want to be remembered. You might not be able to have Bonnie Raitt, Jackson Browne, and Stevie Wonder sing *Amazing Grace* like they did for Stevie Ray Vaughn, but you can include a personal music selection, flower arrangement, and items for the memorial table.

- Traditional music choices include Handel's *Dead March*, Bach's *Toccata and Fugue* in D minor, and Chopin's *Funeral March*.

On the Web

- About.Com—How to Plan a Christian Funeral. **Christianity. About.com/od/christianfuneral/a/funeralplanning.htm**

- The National Funeral Directors Association—This is the largest funeral organization in the world. This site lists consumer resources and gives information on pricing and funeral trends. **NFDA.org**

- Things NOT To Do At A Funeral—A most entertaining article. **HubPages.com/hub/Things-NOT-To-Do-At-A-Funeral**

- WikiHow—How to Conduct a Traditional Protestant Funeral Service. **WikiHow.com/Conduct-a-Traditional-Protestant-Funeral-Service**

A SHAGGY DOG STORY

My friend's father was a dog lover who had many dogs during his life. To honor them, he always had them cremated and put into lovely urns. When he died, his final wishes were to be cremated and have his urn present at his service. As these things happen, the crematorium broke down and my friend's father could not be cremated in time for the service. The family substituted one of the dog urns instead. During the service, each time the minister unknowingly and lovingly placed his hand on the urn, the family had to place their hands over their mouths.

MEMORIAL SERVICE

A memorial service is held without the body present. It is dedicated to the memory of the person and focuses on their values and how they lived their lives. A memorial service:

- Can be held in lieu of a traditional funeral

- Can be held in conjunction with a funeral, such as one held in a different city
- Will usually have a format that is less structured than a traditional service
- Will usually include more attendees participating in readings and remembrances
- Is often used with cremation and before or after the scattering of ashes
- May be also used before or after burial at sea.

Location of Service

- The ceremony can be held almost anywhere.
- Oftentimes, it is held outdoors, near the place where ashes will be or have been scattered.
- The location is usually relevant to the person's life.

Type of Cemetery

- The type of cemetery does not matter since a memorial service is usually not held at a cemetery.

Pros & Cons

- This is a good idea when your body has been donated to science or when ashes will be scattered later.
- It is not for those who leave behind loved ones needing the weight of a traditional service to help with closure.

Costs

A memorial service can be as simple or lavish as you want. It can be held in a garden with a string quartet, champagne, and caviar, or it can be held on a beach at sunset with cold beer. The best memorial service I've heard of recently was held in a field in New Mexico where friends and family gathered for a reading, then watched as a hot air balloon lifted off, sailing toward the San Cristo Mountains to scatter the ashes.

While you do not have most of the standard costs of a traditional funeral, you may need to pay for some or all of the following:

- The location: Will you have to rent a banquet hall?

- Chairs and tables

- Food

- Drink

- Labor for set up, serving the food and drinks, and other tasks

- Music

- Flowers and other decorations

- Eulogist.

Good to Know

If you decide to have a viewing before your memorial service, you should take a look at the extra expense it will involve. At the minimum it will include:

- Embalming: $380–$675, or for disinfecting without embalming $95–$295

- Dressing/Casketing: $160–$490

- Viewing visitation: $175–$490

- Cosmetic preparation: $75–$250

- Burial clothing: $45–$150.

On the Web

- Creative Memorial Service—How to plan a memorial. **MemorialServicePlanning.com**

- Legacy—Explains the difference between a funeral and memorial service. **Connect.Legacy.com/inspire/page/show?id=1984035%3APage%3A6415**

COMMITTAL SERVICE

This ceremony is usually quite small, with only family and close friends attending. It is held at the graveside before the body is buried or at the crematory before the actual cremation.

- The body is present but the casket is usually closed.

- The body is buried or cremated after the service has ended and everyone has departed.

- This service can include a brief reading, prayers, flowers, and music if you can arrange the logistics.

Type of Cemetery

A committal service can be held in any type of cemetery or crematorium.

Pros & Cons

- A committal ceremony is good for people who do not have extended family or friends.

- It's good for someone who does not want to have any fuss.

- It may leave some family members and friends feeling left out.

Costs

The costs for this service are usually less than the traditional funeral or memorial service, basically involving just the burial or cremation costs—especially if you are going to simply have family and friends stand and listen to a reading. You may end up paying for some of the costs associated with a memorial service, such as food and drink or a eulogist.

Good to Know

While this is not a usual custom, you can have a viewing beforehand if you want.

On the Web

- Funeral.Com—This site offers hundreds of funeral links and includes a community bulletin board, as well as business listings and classified ads. **Funeral.com**

- My Name is Brandon—A Christian committal service. **MyNameIsBrandon.Wordpress.com/2007/03/08/youngministerscom-commital-service-1**

ALTERNATIVE SERVICE

As far as I'm concerned, anything you want at your service is fine—as long as it isn't illegal. Release 1,000 white doves, read from Dashiell Hammett's *The Maltese Falcon* or from the poetry of Jack Kerouac. Have a gingerbread house decorating contest. Serve shish kabob sandwiches to be eaten while the Armenian national anthem plays over your casket. Spray the attendees with Silly String. Anything you want goes.

Alternative services may be determined by the location of the service.

- Green or natural burial grounds are often located in open fields or woods. Conservational burial cemeteries are designated nature preserves where the ground is kept in its natural state. Elaborate services with music, tents, and chairs might be difficult and may not be allowed.

- Burial at sea often includes a ceremony on a boat, which has all sorts of limitations, not least of which is seasickness. It may be best to hold off on the tequila sunrises until afterward.

- An at-home burial site should allow for almost any type of ceremony, but the exact location might present its own constraints.

On the Web

- EHow—How to perform a pagan funeral. **EHow.com/how_2075325_perform-pagan-funeral.html**

- Padfield—A funeral service for a non-Christian. **PadField.com/1997/funeral.html**

TYPE OF FORMAT FOR YOUR SERVICE

After you decide which type of service might suit you best, you can choose the format that appeals to you. There are basically four formats. Here are their characteristics:

Religious

- Usually used for traditional services
- Follows prescribed rituals
- Emphasis is on faith and the afterlife
- Usually held in a place of worship

Vietnam Veterans Memorial Paddle-Out, Oceanside, California, Pier & Amphitheater September 30, 2007. *Photograph courtesy of Jerry Anderson*

- Clergy is usually in charge of the service
- Includes religious readings and hymns
- Can be quite formal.

Nonreligious

- Usually used for memorial, committal, and alternative services
- Follows no set rules
- Emphasis is on personality, history, stories, and memories
- Usually held at a personally significant location, but can be held anywhere
- Friends usually officiate but clergy can be included
- May include readings, secular music, and memorabilia
- Is usually semi-formal.

Family gathering

- Usually used for committal services, cremation, and/or scattering of ashes
- Follows no set rules
- Emphasis is on family and the person's place in that family
- Usually held in a family member's home
- A family member usually organizes and runs the gathering
- Includes memories of the person as a family member.

Private

- Follows no set rules
- Can be any type or format
- Good for those wanting a simple format or lower costs
- One focus may be restricting access to the event. If you are famous—this may be the way to go.

Matching Service with Disposition of the Body

The type of service you choose will depend, somewhat, on what you have decided to do with your body. We discussed your options in Chapter 1. Here is a guide to what choices match best with which services:

- With body bequeathal, where your body is donated to medical science or research and you won't get it back, your best choice might be a memorial service.

- Direct disposition, where your body is taken from the place of death directly to the place of burial or cremation, may call for a committal service beforehand or a memorial service afterwards.

- With either above-ground entombment or below-ground burial, you can chose a traditional funeral service, a memorial service, or a committal service at the time of the burial or to be performed at another time.

- Cremation, with scattering of the ashes, goes well with a memorial service.

- A memorial service at another location or a committal service at the site works well with cremation when the ashes will be placed in either a niche in a columbarium or buried.

- You can have a memorial service of any type in any convenient location when your choice is cremation with the ashes being taken home to be kept there.

- With burial at sea, you can have a full or committal service on the boat or a memorial service on the shore.

PRACTICAL CONSIDERATIONS

Location

Consider where your family and friends are located. Will it be a logistical nightmare to have everyone travel to your area for a large funeral? Perhaps a memorial service in one part of the country and a funeral service in the other might be a good idea.

Financial Considerations

How much are you willing to set aside for your final service? Do you have an insurance policy specifically for your funeral? An acquaintance of mine, Fred, died last year. Before his death, he sequestered quite a bit of money for his funeral, a High Episcopal service with printed programs, decorations, tons of flowers, and a memorial display. Yes, Fred put aside quite a bit of change for this final service, but one year later people are still talking about how nice it was.

Religious Considerations

Some people want the church and all its angels present; others would be more comfortable with a ceremony that is humanistic and nonsectarian. My cousin, who is deeply religious, wants a traditional funeral, including a full church service, communion, a eulogy, and the reading of several Bible passages. My good friend, Carol, holds no religious beliefs at all. She says she wants a memorial service that omits Bible readings but includes readings on how to treat other people with respect and compassion.

Consider not only your beliefs, but those of your family and friends. If your spouse is quite religious and you're not, you still might want to have a religious ceremony to please him or her.

Your religion may prescribe that specific events take place in a prearranged order or be quite strict about what you must include. Check with your religious leader to determine what is considered necessary and proper and then include these things on your planning sheet.

YOUR EULOGY

Do not leave the writing of this important remembrance of yourself to just anyone. You are perfectly within your rights to specify who you want to write and read your eulogy. Remember what Oscar Wilde said: "Any fool can make history, but it takes a genius to write it."

Here are some ideas you might want to leave for your eulogist, or to use for writing your own eulogy:

- If you have a theme, it will make it easier for the eulogist. It is also a good way to direct the process of writing it. The theme can be serious or humorous. It can be religious or even sacrilegious, if that is your preference. It can have a nautical, freedom-loving, or artistic bent—whatever fits who you are.

- Things to consider include: how you served your community or the world; your family; how you lived your life; jobs you held; and the places you visited.

- Have a chronological list of important events you want mentioned.

- You don't have to brag, but if you want people to remember the good things that you did in your life, now is the time.

- Provide a list of what was important to you and how your life reflected it.

- Express your dreams, wishes, or goals for those left behind.

- A personal letter from you might be a nice way for you to leave behind a few words of comfort or direction as part of your eulogy.

- A few anecdotes reflecting who you are: like the time you saved that puppy from drowning, or when you leapt tall buildings with a single bound, and definitely when you swam buck-naked in the pond at Woodstock.

- Share a few specific memories with those who might be left standing.

- Find some specific readings or quotes: Pull out some of your old books and look for passages that you might have underlined; the Bible is good for this, as are poetry tomes. You might consider something from the great thirteenth-century Persian poet Rumi.

On the Web

- About.com—How to write a eulogy. **Dying.About.com/od/funeralsandmemorials/ht/write_a_eulogy.htm**

- Different Eulogy Writing Styles and Themes—The title says it all. **EulogySpeech.net/eulogy-writing/Different-Eulogy-Writing-Themes-Styles.shtml**

- Famous Eulogies—Eulogies of famous folks. **EulogyWriters.com/famous-eulogies.html**

- Toastmasters International—Tips on how to give a eulogy. **ToastMasters.org**

BIG FRANK'S BEER SEND-OFF

My cousin-by-marriage was a big, wonderful, warm-hearted guy who loved nothing so much as spending the day with his boat waterskiing. After his death, family and friends met beside the river to toast his memory and regale each other with great stories. Once the stories were finished, the immediate family went out in the boat to scatter his ashes. As luck would have it, the wind picked up and blew his ashes back against the hull. With the boat sitting too high in the water for them to reach down and splash the side of the boat, they decided it would be fitting to open a bottle of beer and wash his ashes into the river. The onshore crowd applauded.

THE VISITATION

At a visitation, the immediate family gathers to receive condolences from extended family, friends, and acquaintances. A visitation usually involves the following:

- It is usually held in the funeral home or a church, but a visitation can also be held in the home of a family member or a friend.

- It takes place on a specific day, with a specified time.

- It can be as formal or relaxed as you want it to be.

- It can be as simple as having the family seated about casually, with a guest book to be signed at the entrance, or more formal, with a receiving line.

- It can include a brief ceremony.

- It can have the casket present, either open or closed. It is up to you.

A traditional service usually calls for a formal visitation at the funeral home or church with a receiving line or brief ceremony. A memorial service usually involves a more informal visitation held at the home of your family or the home of a friend.

Costs

Using a funeral home entails room rental and attending costs, which can run anywhere from $150 to $500. A cost-effective alternative would be to have the visitation at your church or at the home of your family or a friend; but if you want the casket there, you will have to pay transportation costs, which can range from $300 to $800.

THE VIEWING

Makes your toes curl, right? I know, mine too. A viewing may be included in your visitation...or not. A viewing means having an open casket where people file by and pay their respects. Singer-songwriter Hank Williams lay in state for two days with an open casket while over 20,000 people walked by to pay their respects. In Moderna, Italy, over 10,000 mourners paid tribute to opera icon Luciano Pavarotti, filing past his red, veil-draped casket.

This one is totally your choice. Everybody has his or her own opinions about having an open casket and these opinions are usually quite strong. Some people say folks need to see the body for closure to help them finally accept that the person is dead. I say I'll take the funeral director's word on it.

My Aunt Martha was the exact opposite. When her mother went to the Great Beyond, she wanted that casket open and she wanted to present a good look. Heck, Aunt Martha even checked to see that the body had on proper underpants. Really. Some people say that an open casket gives them nightmares, but the sight of my aunt patting the face of her beloved mother as she lay in her casket was a picture that comforted the entire family. So it's your choice. As for me, nobody has ever been able to style my hair properly and I'm not about to have everyone remember me going to my final reward looking like a dance party extra on *The Patty Duke Show*.

Things to Consider:

- Hair: It would be best to leave a picture of how you want your hair done.

- Makeup: Again, a picture would be good, or perhaps you could use instructions saying, "Please make my complexion look smooth for once."

- Clothing: Indicate the type of clothes you want—formal, dress suit, church dress, or casual. If you want something special, write it down. Full-dress military uniforms are a favorite choice, formal evening gowns are often considered, and some women want to be buried in their wedding dresses, although what that says about the state of their marriages is beyond me. If anybody puts me in pantyhose, I'm going to haunt them forever.

- Jewelry: If you want to be all gussied up, great. Just be sure to leave instructions as to whether or not the jewelry should be taken off and to whom it should be given (usually the executor of your estate). In my mind, there's nothing worse than burying a perfectly good diamond ring.

Costs

Here are ballpark figures of expenses you might incur with a viewing.

Viewing at a funeral home:

- Dressing/Casketing: $160– $490

- Viewing/Visitation: $175–$490.

Viewing at a church or family home (if state regulations allow it) will also include:

- Hearse: $175–$400

- Transportation fee: $160–$395.

Good to Know

Now you can look good at your viewing! Plastic surgery after death is the new fashion trend. Read the Inquisitr's article titled: "Wanna Look Good for Your Funeral? Plastic Surgery after Death the New Fashion Trend": **Inquisitr.com/11412/look-good-for-your-funeral-plastic-surgery-after-death-the-new-fashion-trend**.

THE WAKE

A wake is another form of a visitation, but is more informal and, from all reports, much more fun. I'm sure everyone has heard about the wake where they ran out of chairs and had to prop the casket in a corner, leaning it up against the wall. A wake generally:

- Is held before any formal ceremony

- Often involves having the body present for viewing

- Usually takes place in a club, a hall, or at someone's home

- Always involves food and drink and much storytelling

- Employs a friend of the deceased as the master of ceremonies

- Includes a memorial table with pictures, trophies, and the like.

THE RECEPTION

A reception can be many things to many people, but the important thing is that it can be a place where your loved ones begin the healing process. Astonishing things happen at receptions. My young cousin was so moved by the funeral of her uncle that she sat next to the preacher in the living room where the reception was held. Later she joined the pastor's church.

At another reception held after the death of a childhood friend, two people who hadn't seen each other for twenty years became reacquainted and began dating.

Receptions usually follow the format of the service. A traditional service might have a quiet reception, while a reception with a festive air might follow other types of services. However, you can always mix and match. Receptions:

- Are usually held directly after the funeral or interment

- Can be held in almost any venue

- Can be quiet and traditional or rowdy and irreverent

- Allow family and friends to share their sorrow and begin to heal

- Are where people celebrate your life with laughter and fond memories.

A friend from my rock-n-roll radio days had a mix-and-match service and reception. For religious and family considerations, she planned a traditional funeral. For the reception that followed she honored her friends and the life she had led with a party featuring music, food, laughter, and remembrances. It was loud, it was fun, and even the older, more traditional family members and friends got into the swing of things—after overcoming their initial shock, that is.

You can always go out with a bang, placing your cremated remains in a fireworks display. *Photograph courtesy of Angels Flight (Angels-Flight.net)*

Location

Your reception can literally be held anywhere you want: on a beach, at a park, at your favorite restaurant, at the top of Yosemite's Half Dome. Make sure you include instructions for anything special that you would like.

For instance, a friend of mine who was a sailing fanatic had his sailboat anchored where everyone at the reception could see it. The boat's flags were flying in a configuration indicating that the captain was coming home, into port. That brought both tears and smiles.

Costs

How much to set aside for your reception depends on what type of reception you want to have, where it will be held, and what food or drinks will be served. Mostly, the costs are the same as for any other party.

On the Web

- EHow—How to prepare food for a funeral reception. **EHow.com/how_2085890_prepare-food-funeral-reception.html**

- My Funky Funeral—This site can help you choose your music, and offers samples and download capability. **MyFunkyfuneral.com/song.php**

It's My Party ...

Think of your planning of your celebration as a final gift to those you have left behind. If you don't tell them, how are they going to know that you want a traditional funeral with all the pomp and circumstance, a formal viewing, and a quiet reception? On the other hand, how would they ever guess that at your open-casket viewing, you want a movement sensor that sets off a tape player so, when someone passes by to pay their respects, your voice will come booming out, saying things like "What have you done with your hair?" or "Did you ever return that book I lent you?" (My friend

George swears he is going to do this, but then George worked for the IRS—go figure.) Remember, you are doing a good thing! Roy and Dale would agree.

This link sends you to a great Free Library article by Cynthia L. Webb, "Fans Bid Happy Trails to Roy Rogers": **www.thefreelibrary. com/FAMILY%2c+FANS+BID+ADIEU+TO+COWBOY+ROY+ ROGERS%3b+HEARSE+CIRCLES+MUSEUM.-a064792904.**

HELP ME CHOOSE

Which of the following statements are true for you?

- A funeral will be important to my family and friends.
- I am, or my family is, quite traditional.
- A service without my body in attendance makes sense.
- I think an additional service where I lived or worked would be nice.
- I am religious and gain great comfort from my religion.
- I lean more toward humanistic ideals than religious ideals.
- I like big gatherings and a roaring-good party.
- I like things calm and quiet.
- I'd like an open place for people to gather before the service.
- Dude, I'm famous. It all has to be private.
- An open coffin gives me the willies.
- I want to add some sass to my final going away; watch out attendees!
- I have money set aside for an expensive wake or reception.

CHAPTER 6

I Heard It Through the Grapevine: So Who Wants or Needs to Know?

Eula! Look at this. Right here. It's Miss Victoria. She's dead!" Eula looked up from her ironing, "When'd that happen? It wasn't in the church bulletin." Linda Mae poked the newspaper with her finger, "I know. Says here the funeral was yesterday. Yesterday! Can you believe it? And they didn't even have the manners to tell us! Just wait until I call Julia. I bet they didn't tell her either! Some people just don't have any bringing-up!"

As Karl Malden would say, "Don't let this happen to you." When you finally shuffle off this mortal coil, people are going to need to know: family, friends, business associates, and perhaps an old lover or two. The how, why, when, and where of proper notification is an important and necessary part of the mourning ritual. After all, you may be dead, but you still have to mind your manners.

This chapter will help you decide whom to tell and when. Stop and think for a minute: Family and friends should probably be phoned immediately, business clients may appreciate a printed announcement, and you may want to make a lasting announcement via a memorial marker. We will also talk about the things that should be included in your obituary and help you plan what you want mentioned and what you might want left out ("Senator Quagmire, once indicted for perjury...").

Your Obituary

The root of the word "obituary" is the Latin word "obitus" which means "departure" or "encounter." This is where the rest of the world gets to know that you have "left the building." There are three types of formal death notification. Sometimes these terms are used interchangeably.

A death notice is the first announcement of a person's death. It is much shorter than an obituary and gives minimal information. A death notice basically contains the person's name, city of birth, and time and place of death. Some include the cause of death. In addition, the time, date, and location of the funeral are stated. Often, a death notice is placed in the paper a day or two prior to the publication of the more lengthy obituary.

An obituary is a notice, usually in a newspaper, that announces a person's death and includes an extended account of the person's life and a list of family members. An obituary is often written by the funeral home or mortuary, but it can also be written by a family member, friend, or even the deceased—prior to dying, of course.

A "funeral obituary" is a final notice that announces the death of someone and explains when and where the funeral took place. Usually published first in the funeral program, a funeral obituary is often then placed online, along with an extended biography.

Pros and Cons

- A published obituary can alert family, friends, business associates, and casual acquaintances about your departure.

- On the down side, concern about identity theft is causing some to recommend omitting information such as the date of birth in an obituary. The Identity Theft Resource Center states: "Identity thieves obtain information about deceased individuals in various ways. They may watch the obituaries, steal death certificates, or even get the information from websites that offer the

Social Security Death Index file." Visit their website for excellent guidance. The Identity Theft Resource Center: **idtheftcenter.org/artman2/publish/c_guide/Fact_Sheet_117_ IDENTITY_THEFT_AND_THE_DECEASED_-_PREVEN- TION_AND_VICTIM_TIPS.shtml**.

OH MY!

This obituary of Dolores Aguilar was published on August 16 and 17, 2008, in the *Vallejo Times-Herald*:

Dolores Aguilar, born in 1929 in New Mexico, left us on August 7, 2008.

Dolores had no hobbies, made no contribution to society and rarely shared a kind word or deed in her life. I speak for the majority of her family when I say her presence will not be missed by many, very few tears will be shed, and there will be no lamenting over her passing.

Her family will remember Dolores and amongst ourselves we will remember her in our own way, which were mostly sad and troubling times throughout the years. We may have some fond memories of her and perhaps we will think of those times too. But I truly believe at the end of the day ALL of us will really only miss what we never had, a good and kind mother, grandmother, and great-grand-mother. I hope she is finally at peace with herself.

As for the rest of us left behind, I hope this is the begin-ning of a time of healing and learning to be a family again. There will be no service, no prayers and no closure for the family she spent a lifetime tearing apart. We cannot come together in the end to see to it that her grandchildren and great-grandchildren can say their goodbyes. So I say here for all of us, GOOD BYE, MOM.

Costs

You may want to have your obituary run in more than one newspaper. Here are some ideas about the costs:

- Most newspapers charge by the inch or per line. Major metropolitan area papers can charge up to $100 per inch for weekend editions and over $150 more for including a photograph.

- Medium sized newspapers will likely charge anywhere from $10–$15 per line and something less than $150 additional for a photo.

- Small newspapers will often run an obituary for free.

- Many papers will publish newsworthy obituaries (public figures, prominent locals, and celebrities) for free.

- Many larger papers offer online-only death notices for a fee. Other smaller papers have a no-fee e-newspaper service.

How Do I Do It?

First, call the newspapers and get their prices. This will give you an idea about the amount of information you want included in your obituary. Next, you fill out the worksheets in the back of the book (or download them at **DeathForBeginners.com**) and designate whom you would like to write your obituary.

You can also write your own obituary or at least the major part of it. There are some very good reasons you might want to do this:

- It is your chance to tell others what you want them to know about you.

- You will gain peace of mind knowing that you have had your say.

- Your family and friends will get a kick out of reading it and knowing you wrote it.

- You get to evaluate your life while you still have a chance to accomplish some unmet goals and forgotten intentions.

- You do not want someone writing personal details that take that one step beyond insightful into inappropriate. For example, having the cousin who never liked you write, "Having married five times, Karen greatly enjoyed her life despite that unfortunate incident in Tijuana...."

Here are some suggestions to get you started on writing your own obituary:

- Make a list of things you want people to remember about you to use as a starting point. Include your accomplishments.

- Concentrate on focusing on the life lived rather than a notice of death.

- Write short anecdotes of special events in your life.

- Make a timeline of your life year-by-year so you don't leave anything out.

- Ask some good friends what you should list.

- Go online and read other obituaries.

A good template for a self-written obituary might look like this:

- Section one—full name, date and place of birth

- Section two—list of immediate family and any predeceased close relatives

- Section three—main events of your life, jobs or businesses, military service, memberships, awards, accomplishments, and great passions

- Section four—education, degrees, hobbies, interests

- Section five—charities or memorial funds to which you wish people to make donations

- Be sure to attach the photo you want used.

Good to Know

- Your obituary should be given to several local newspapers to ensure that as many people as possible become aware of your death.

- If you have lived in several different areas, it would be good idea to have your obituary sent to those local newspapers.

- Don't forget notification on your Facebook or LinkedIn (or similar social media website) pages.

- Some newspapers require an accompanying death certificate if someone other than a funeral home submits the obituary. Apparently some people have tried to supply obituaries of former spouses who were not deceased at the time. I know, go ahead and make up your own joke here.

On the Web

- Obituaries Help—A state-by-state list of newspapers that publish free obituaries online. **ObituariesHelp.org/free_obituaries_hub.html**

- PoynterOnline—An article about writing your own obituary. **Poynter.org/content/content_view.asp?id=99020**

- The Remembering Site—Gives you topics and questions to ask yourself to get the writing process started. **TheRememberingSite.org/view.php**

- Elvis Pelvis—As a break, check out this website about "Dead Musicians...and How They Got that Way." You can search by cause of death such as "not eating." **ElvisPelvis.com/fullerup.htm**

- Facebook deceased member notice link. **FaceBook.com/help/search.php?hq=deceased**

- LinkedIn deceased member notice link. **LinkedIn.custhelp.com**

- MySpace deceased member notice link. **Faq.MySpace.com/app/answers/detail/a_id/369**

The "A" List

When you die, there will be plenty of people who need to be notified. The worksheet section in the back of the book has a list for you to use, but the notification process will go something like this:

- First phone calls—immediate family and friends

- Second phone calls—pastor, rabbi or spiritual guidance provider, funeral provider, a trusted neighbor, and the friend who can take care of anything

- Personal e-mail—sent to extended family and friends

- Formal e-mail—sent to distant family, casual friends, and selected business associates

- Formal death notice—a few lines in the paper announcing funeral arrangements and a phone number or Web address for further information

- Third round of phone calls—to anyone with whom you may have had standing appointments: hairdresser, volunteer committee, therapist, social clubs

- Formal obituary—sent to local newspapers

- Web sites—your obituary on your social and business web sites

- Written formal notices—to business contacts, financial institutions, government agencies, and so forth

Give the worksheet (see back of the book)—filled out with names and contact information—to the person who will be handling this since you won't be able to do it.

Notifications You Can Make from the Beyond—Well Sort of

Oh yes, you read that right. Thanks to the Internet, you can now send e-mails to people after you are dead. This is a perfectly wonderful way to let people know that they will always be in your heart.

It is also a perfectly good way to scare them to death. On one hand, I think it is a lovely thing to do; on the other hand, it creeps me out a little. Some people just need to, you know, stay dead. Either way, it is something to consider in this age of the World Wide Web. Two sites are worth checking out if you are considering doing this.

"My Last Email" is a site that encourages you to never leave anything unsaid. On this site, you can create an online memorial where messages can posthumously be sent to family and friends. You can also leave letters, photographs, or a video message that can be accessed by family and friends. A simple package is free. You pay for added options. **MyLastEmail.com**

"Future Me" is a very simple site where you fill out a form and your e-mails are sent out at a future date. The twist here is you can designate your e-mail as "public, but anonymous," and it will be included in the public letters section. Man, talk about a way to spend a rainy day reading some fascinating stuff. It works, it's simple, and there is no charge. **FutureMe.org**

THE COWBOY'S PRAYER

Oh Lord, I reckon I'm not much just by myself.

I fail to do a lot of things I ought to do.

But Lord, when trails are steep and passes high,

Help me to ride it straight the whole way through.

And when in the falling dusk I get the final call,

I do not care how many flowers they send—

Above all else the happiest trail would be

For You to say to me, "Let's ride, My friend."

Amen

—Roy Rogers gravestone, Sunset Hills Memorial Park, Apple Valley, California

Notifications That Last—Memorial Markers

This is the lasting way of putting people on notice. With a memorial marker, you tell people that you were indeed, at one time, here on the planet. You can set a memorial marker just about any place you want, as long as the property owner agrees with its placement. Memorial markers range from headstones in traditional cemeteries to private garden markers, to plaques on undersea reefs, to pages on the Internet. The latest rage is to have a solar-powered panel containing a multimedia tribute to the deceased mounted on the monument or memorial marker. Who says baby boomers are self-absorbed? Just think, you can make your own tribute before you die and include all of those moments when you looked really skinny. Be sure you let friends and family know exactly what you want inscribed on your marker. Buddy Holly has his real name "Holley" spelled correctly on his marker, along with the depiction of a guitar leaning against a Doric column.

Memorial Markers—At the Gravesite

Memorial markers used at gravesites can be traditional, nontraditional, homemade, or simply unusual. It all depends on where your body is buried and what you want.

Traditional Cemetery

If you are being buried in a traditional cemetery, the markers are usually limited to pillow stones, statues, or markers that are set flat against the ground. You will have to follow the cemetery guidelines and your particular cemetery may not want an unusual or homemade marker on the grounds.

Nontraditional Cemetery

As we've discussed, nontraditional cemeteries include natural burial grounds, eco-forests, conservation burial grounds, and home sites. Each of these sites comes with its own special limitations.

- Natural burial ground—These sites often use grave markers that don't intrude on the landscape. These natural markers can include shrubs and trees or an engraved flat stone native to the area. Records are kept of the exact location of the grave and sometimes a GPS system is used for visitors to locate the marker.

- Eco-forest— Sometimes in natural burial sites where ashes are placed beneath trees, a marker is placed on the tree; but most sites will not allow markers. Instead, records are kept of the exact location. A GPS system is often used for individual site location.

- Conservational burial ground—As the greenest of all burial sites, no markers are allowed and even visitation is limited. Records are kept of the exact location and, again, a GPS system may be used.

- Home site—With these sites, you can do exactly what you want, as long as you follow any local statutes.

Costs

Charges for a traditional cemetery marker include construction, installation, and maintenance. That said, you can pay as much as you want for a monument that is as elaborate as you feel you need. Bronze plaques that lie flat against the ground run about $900. Prices for statues may run from about $200 for simple plaster or cement models to very expensive ones carved from marble. It's up to you. Spend away.

Veterans

The Department of Veterans Affairs will furnish a government headstone or marker at no charge for veterans. If you place it in a private cemetery, you may have to pay setting fees. Complete information is available at **www.CEM.VA.gov/cem/hm_hm.asp**.

How Do I Do It?

Learn what is out there and compare prices. If you use a funeral home or cemetery, it will have suggestions. I suggest you go online to find the best bargain. There are some great deals on traditional markers.

Good to Know

While cemeteries are not governed by the FTC's "Funeral Rule," unless they sell both funeral goods and funeral services, most cemeteries:

- Will not object to your buying a headstone from others

WRITE YOUR OWN EPITAPH

An epitaph is a short, concise, lasting record of who you were. Someone else may pen one for you but, if you write your own, you have a chance to leave a succinct message for those you know and those you don't know. You might want to visit several websites to see what others wrote. An excellent site is Famous Quotes—**FamousQuotes.me.uk/epitaphs**.

Some examples:

- Ludwig van Beethoven: "Friends applaud, the comedy is finished."

- Wild Bill Hickok: "Pard, we will meet again in the Happy Hunting Ground to part no more."

- Bette Davis: "She Did It the Hard Way."

- Mel Blanc: "That's all, folks."

- And, of course, last, but certainly not least, William Shakespeare: "Good frend for Jesus sake forbeare to dig the dust enclosed heare. Blest be ye man yt spares thes stones and curst be he yt moves my bones."

- Will routinely accept delivery of the headstone and install it for you for a reasonable fee—usually between $100–$400

- Will not allow self-installation—these things are often heavy!

- Will have restrictions regarding size, color, and wording but will follow generally accepted practices.

National cemeteries have strict veteran marker guidelines.

A glowing tribute. Think about a translucent cast-glass memorial instead of a traditional granite or bronze headstone. *Photograph courtesy of Lundgren Monuments (LundgrenMonuments.com)*

On the Web

- Memorials.com—This site has statues of angels, with prices starting under $200. **Memorials.com/statues.php**

- VidsStone—This business offers a solar-powered "Serenity Panel," containing a seven-inch LCD panel that plays a five to eight minute video available for mounting on your memorial stone. **VidStone.com**

Got You Pegged

In the old days, people carved special symbols onto memorial markers, indicating the nature of the deceased. Can you imagine some that might be carved today? The Haunt Masters Club has an extensive list: **HauntMastersClub.com/tools/symbols.html**. Here are some:

- Tree trunk = life cut short

- Lamb = innocence

- Hourglass = the swiftness of time

- Lily = purity

- Weeping willow = grief

- Dolphin = salvation

- Crown = reward

- Shell = resurrection.

MEMORIAL MARKERS—NOT AT THE GRAVESITE

Some of us will want to place our markers somewhere other than on top of our graves. This may be the case when you are buried in a nontraditional cemetery that does not allow markers, when your ashes will be scattered, when you are being buried at sea, or when you are donating your body and it will not be returned. This means that without gravesite limitations and cemetery rules to follow, you can have a really cool marker.

The main consideration here is where you want your memorial marker to be placed. Here are some ideas to get you thinking:

- Charity placement—There are plenty of private hospitals, hospices, nature trails, and so forth that sell markers for walls and walkways that include your name, dates of birth and death, and a small personal note. You may be able to donate a chunk of money to a municipal garden, swimming pool, or health center and have your memorial on a big honking brass plaque placed there.

- You can have a very nice garden marker placed at your home or in a relative's garden.

- If you are scattered at sea, perhaps you can have your marker placed near the shore. Why not offer to help pay for a period of maintenance on a fishing pier and have a marker placed on the railing? I know several people who are having their markers placed in a boatyard near the docks.

- You could have a marker placed somewhere in nature. You will likely need to ask permission, but many people want a small marker placed where their ashes were scattered or where they had happy memories.

There are all types of memorial markers available. Those that you might use for the garden are shaped like stones or boulders. If you want to be understated, you can use a simple brass plaque, perhaps attached to a tree or the side of a building. A bench might be a good choice if you want your memorial marker placed in a park. You may choose a memorial statue to be placed on your family property or elsewhere, with proper permission.

On the Web

- Ever Life Memorials—Memorial trees for outside gardens: $677. **EverLifeMemorials.com/memorial-trees-s/102.htm**

- Valley Monuments—They have exact replicas of boulders and trees that begin at around $750. **ValleyMonuments.com**

MEMORIALS—ON THE WEB

Who says the Internet isn't great? Where else can you live forever? All you have to do is get on the Internet and Google "Internet Memorials" to get started.

Non-fee Websites

Simple, non-fee sites let you post limited information and text. Some have a specific time period during which information will be posted; others will retain the information until the site shuts down. Some have you sharing a page with other folks and others let you have your own personal page that includes a guestbook, a few pictures, and a way to donate to a charity. Here are some examples:

- Angel Families Online—**AngelFamiliesOnline.com**

- Cemetery.org—**Cemetery.org**

- Gone Too Soon—**GoneTooSoon.org**

- In Memoriam—**Hosting411.info/memorial**.

Fee-Charging Sites

These sites offer more interactive options. Most will give you a free two-week trial, while others will let you have a webpage free for a month or two and then ask that you join. Well, maybe not ask *you*, but ask the person you designate. Some charge as much as $40 per month, while others have a one-time fee of $50–$70. Some will let you join for a month-to-month fee ranging from $5 to $10 per month. They often include these options:

- You can create a custom design, including links to other sites.

- Photos, video files, audio files, and slideshows may be posted on the site.

- Visitors may leave messages, contact each other, make donations to charities, send personalized e-mails to family members, and invite others to visit the site.

The following are some examples of sites:

- iLasting: **ILasting.com**

- Last Memories: **Last-Memories.com**

- Memorial Websites: **MemorialWebsites.legacy.com**.

Social Networking Sites

Facebook—Provides a service where a limited Facebook memorial page will replace the user's wall information and remain online for about thirty days. The person you designate to handle this will need your login and password information. Here is the Facebook link to get started: **FaceBook.com/help/search.php?hq=deceased**.

Myspace—Will delete the profile for you if the person you have designated to handle this is a next of kin, has your MySpace friend ID, and e-mails them proof of death, such as an obituary or death certificate. Here is the link to get started: **FAQ.Myspace.com/app/answers/detail/a_id/369**.

HELP ME CHOOSE

Your selections from the options below will tell you which choice might be best for you.

- I want lots of people to know about my funeral plans.

- I would have liked to have my own reality show.

- I want to live forever in cyberspace.

- I am a private person and others don't need to know details of my life and death.
- I am very traditional.
- I am not traditional.
- I want to make sure my eulogy says what I want it to say.
- I want to make a statement with my memorial marker.
- I have x-amount of money set aside for a memorial marker.
- A memorial placed at a special place would mean a lot to me.
- I'm going to be scattered and I don't care about a marker.

CHAPTER 7

The Long and Winding Road: The Paper Trail

Hovering around the bed, the greedy family waits. The frail old woman gives one last smile and gently passes away. Fleeing the deathwatch, shoving their way into the library, the family gathers impatiently. The attorney looks around, clears his throat, and informs them that the whole of the old woman's estate has been left to a kindly kitchen maid. Ain't death grand? For once, you get to have the last say and no one can stop you. Revenge and reward can both be quite sweet.

But it can't be sweet if no one can find your will or your other important papers. Remember your high school locker? How you fumbled with the lock, opened the door, and everything came piling out onto the floor? How you gave your friend the combination because he needed your notes from history class but he couldn't find them in the chaos? Has anything changed? Probably not. If you're like most of us, you think you have everything organized, when nothing could be further from the truth.

In this chapter, we're going to discuss the purpose of a will, why you need one, and what can happen if you die without one. Do you really want to be like James Brown, the Godfather of Soul? He died on Christmas Day, 2006, and with all of the family wrangling it took two months to bury him and almost three years to finally settle his estate. No way was he singing "I Feel Good." We're also going to figure out how to blaze a neat and orderly trail to your will and other important papers. We will talk about how to organize your important papers and where they should be located. We will also list the requirements for the death certificate. We will discuss death benefits and provide lists for you to consider. So, before your feet fly over your head—let's get started.

Your Will

A will is a legal document that declares your wishes concerning distribution of your assets, the care of any minor children or other dependents you may have, and the care of your pets after you die. Properly executed, it is a legal document that must be followed. So you really do get to have the last say.

I am not an attorney nor is this legal advice. Legal requirements differ from state to state. Below we will just talk about some general concepts. Be sure to obtain professional legal advice when preparing your will.

The Purpose of a Will

A properly executed will can save your family time, money, and anguish, and it can give you peace of mind. It can also:

- Protect your loved ones by making sure the assets you have acquired over the years are passed on as you wish them to be

- Facilitate the transfer of these assets and give you the choice of the person who will administer that transfer

- Protect your children's future by allocating assets for education and (if necessary) appointing legal guardianship

- Protect the well-being of beloved pets

- Protect the interests of all family members if you are in a second (or third or fourth or fifth or...) marriage. If you leave a previous will in effect and do not change it to reflect your new circumstances, that will is still a valid and effective document. However, your new spouse's rights and the court's ability to modify distribution to take into account any children born after the will was made can affect this. This is why this situation is a staple of television soap operas—much drama, pain, and anguish.

- Protect the interest of a partner or "de facto spouse" who may not have automatic entitlement to your estate.

Types of Wills

- Self-Proving/Testamentary Will—The best will around and the one you want. This is the traditional type of will, a formally-prepared document that is signed in the presence of witnesses and abides by all state rules and regulations.

- Holographic Will—A handwritten will without the presence of witnesses. These are only recognized in a few states and rarely hold up in court. You do not want to go the cocktail napkin route.

- Oral Will—A will, or testament, spoken before a witness. Like the holographic will, these are only recognized in a few states and even then usually only under a few extenuating circumstances such as imminent death.

- Video Will—A video made in which the deceased reads his properly executed will and explains why he left what to whom. This could be fun. It could also be used if cousin Ethel tries to challenge the will. Make sure you use the latest technology. Videotape and other mediums degrade, so, if you have already recorded yours, transfer it to the most modern media such as a CD or DVD disk and don't forget to make a copy to store in your safe deposit box.

- Living Will—A living will has nothing to do with your assets. A living will states your wishes regarding medical care concerning life support should you become debilitated. I encourage everyone to consider having such a will. You don't want cousin Ethel pulling the plug too quickly, do you?

For good advice on living wills, see this article by the Mayo Clinic staff: **MayoClinic.com/health/living-wills/HA00014**.

What Is a Valid Will?

A valid will is a will that is accepted by the court. Once accepted, it will be put into effect by granting "probate," which means the court accepts the will as valid and approves of how your assets will be distributed. A valid will usually:

- Needs to be in writing, either handwritten, typed, or printed

- Has to be signed with your signature at the end of the document

- Has to be witnessed and signed by at least two other people. These people have to be present at the time of your signing, acknowledge in writing that they were present, and sign the will in your presence as witnesses.

WHY YOU NEED A WILL

Well, duh. Do you want all of your assets going to someone you don't like, or your ex-spouse, or perhaps divided among some distant, toothless cousins? Don't be lame and say, "There's always time to do this later." Sometimes there's not. Gulp.

WHEN YOU DIE WITHOUT A WILL

When you kick off and haven't taken the time to record your wishes, the state takes control of your assets and distributes them using a fixed formula that varies by state. A court will generally appoint someone to administer the estate and require that this person be paid out of the estate's assets. This is called dying "intestate." I call it dying "insane." Even if you want your property to go to the people who would receive it under the state distribution scheme, you can, with a will, save a number of expenses of state administration, such as limiting the compensation for the person administering the estate and eliminating the requirement that the estate buy an insurance policy to back up the administration of the estate.

There is no reason to not have a will. Here are some examples of what can happen if you don't:

- Survivors may not have a say in the distribution

- You lose the ability to make specific gifts and to divide your assets unequally among your heirs.

- If a spouse and children survive you, the state will generally divide the assets equally among them and the spouse may have to sell the family home to pay the children.

"…. AND TO MY WIFE, ELIZABETH, WHO HATED MY GUTS, I LEAVE MY LARGE INTESTINE."

www.CartoonStock.com

- If you have real property in two states, the property will most likely be divided using two different sets of rules.

- Your heirs will not receive the full amount of your estate. Probating an estate without a will is significantly more expensive (read: "lawyers take a cut") than probating an estate with a will, and the costs are subtracted from the estate.

- If you die without parents, spouse, or children, your assets will go to your siblings and half-siblings equally.

A TALE SAD BUT TRUE

A friend of mine found out that he had AIDS and within several quick months he became seriously ill. Refusing to face reality, he did not make a will. When he died, his home, vacation home, dog, money, and all belongings, including expensive antiques, went to a relative who always scolded him about his lifestyle. My friend's partner of over twenty years was forced out of the home they shared, with nothing but his clothes.

HEIRS AND BENEFICIARIES

You can leave your property to anyone you wish, with a few exceptions that vary among states. For example:

- Some states will not let you disinherit your spouse. A surviving spouse might have a right to a part of the estate regardless of the will.

- Some states have limitations regarding the amount you can leave to charity if you have a surviving spouse or children. Other states have laws regarding charity gifts if you die within a specific time after making the bequests.

- Some states will let you disinherit your children, but you have to specifically state the conditions in the will.

CONTENTS OF A WILL

Just about everything and anything you own can be included in your will. The worksheets in the back of the book provide a list that will get you started on this process.

THE EXECUTOR

Your executor is the person, appointed either by you or, if you die without a will (which is not going to happen, right?), appointed by the court. Your executor has many duties, including being charged with:

- Making sure all of your assets in the will are accounted for
- Administering your estate and making sure your wishes, as stated in your will, are carried out
- Paying debts and taxes
- Handling all court proceedings
- Making funeral arrangements.

Some states allow the court to disqualify your executor if it deems your selection unfit or unable to carry out his or her duties. Your executor should:

- Meet your state's age requirement
- Have no felony convictions
- Be responsible and trustworthy
- Have the time to devote to the task
- Be organized and have access to good advisors
- Perhaps not be a family member if your will is complicated due to family conflicts
- Perhaps not be a business associate if your will involves business interests.

You should always ask permission of the person you want as your executor beforehand and choose an alternate. You should also make provisions for the executor to be paid.

Costs

Costs for drawing up a do-it-yourself will range from free to around $40 for software like Online Quicken WillMaker Plus, if you wish to use the Internet. An attorney will likely charge several hundred dollars. It's up to you. I'd go with an attorney unless your assets are minimal and your heirs few.

How Do I Do It?

Begin by completing the lists that are included in the worksheet section in the back of the book and by completing the following tasks. This assignment will help you organize your thoughts. Even if you already have a will, take a look at the list anyway. You might find something you want to add or delete.

- Make a list of people to whom you want to leave your property.

- Make a second list of other family and friends. This will help you remember someone you may have left out.

- Chose alternate beneficiaries in case the original beneficiary dies. For example, you leave everything to your spouse and you both die together, who gets what then?

- Look at the requirements for an executor. List several names. Remember you will need to name an alternate.

- If you have minor children, make a list of possible guardians, with pros and cons for each person.

- Estimate the value of your estate to get an idea of the amount that you will be leaving behind.

- Look at the worksheets listing insurance policies, annuities, and other benefits to get a good idea of who will be getting the benefits and how much they will receive. This may cause you to revise your original thoughts.

- Make a list of your assets, being sure to include your home, land, co-ops, vacation houses, high-ticket electronics, vehicles, boats, jewelry, contents of safe deposit box, artwork, family heirlooms, and sentimental items. The worksheets will help you with this.

- Take time to walk through your house, closets, and attic with a notepad. You will find things you forgot to put on your list.

Good to Know

- A person may change a will as often as he or she desires. Changes are made by either executing a new will or by executing a legal addition, or amendment, called a codicil.

- A properly drawn and executed will is good until it is changed or revoked.

- You can have more than one executor, each working with a different section of your will.

- In some states, if you die without a will, your divorced former spouse can still inherit your estate because a divorce does not automatically cancel a will. Just imagine that fur fight!

On the Web

- Better Business Bureau—You can check to see if the charity you are giving to is endorsed by the Better Business Bureau. **BBB.org/us/charity**

- Do Your Own Will—Make your will online for free. **DoYourOwnWill.com**

- Read about wills—This web site discusses different types of wills. **Wills-Probate.Lawyers.com/Will-Basics.html**

- Research laws and lawyers—This web site lists lawyers, laws, and resources by state.
  Research.Lawyers.com/State-Law-And-Agencies.html

THE DREADED DIVIDE

"... and all other Property to be divided equally among my heirs."
This sentence has caused a multitude of heartbreaks, hard feelings, and long-standing family feuds. The division of personal possessions usually has less to do with monetary worth and more to do with sentimental value or the continuation of a fight that started at Christmas dinner twenty-five years ago. Heaven help us: Let the fisticuffs over Grandmother's old baking pan begin.

To avoid such dustups, here are some creative giving strategies designed to distribute one's personal belongings such as furniture, china, jewelry, and that baking pan:

- Sentimental Auction. Each heir is given a certain number of credits, often in the form of Monopoly money, and allowed to go through the house and write down bids for each item. Each bid can be adjusted up to a certain time. The high bid gets the item. No one can bid more than the total amount of the credits or Monopoly money they are given.

- Silent Auction. The same as the sentimental auction but the bids are sealed, often being placed in a covered box located beside the item. The advantage of a silent auction is that heirs can bid without the others knowing what they bid on or the amount. Keeps down the squabbling.

- Round Robin. Items are set up and categorized by monetary value, size, type, and sentimental value. For each round of selection, heirs draw numbers from a hat to see who goes first, second, and so on. This can be done for an entire house, where each round is simply held in a different room.

- Fishing. The names of the items are written on pieces of paper. Heirs take turns drawing them from a hat.

- Treasure Hunt. This can be used when there is a hotly disputed one-of-a-kind item such as an engagement ring. An independent party will hide the object and provide clues to its location. A timer should be used. A coin may be flipped if both siblings land at the location simultaneously.

- Low Number Wins. Count the number of items to be divided. Each heir receives that amount of slips of paper with their name on each slip and each slip numbered from one to the total number of items. Heirs walk around and for each item they place a slip in the envelope beside the item. Number One means it is that heir's most desired item. When the envelopes are opened, the slip with the lowest number goes to that heir. For duplicate low numbers, heirs can draw from a hat or flip a coin.

- First Come, First Serve. All heirs make a list of items they want. Any item on just one list and not on any others goes to that person. The list is then divided into slips of paper. Each heir draws a number. Number One gets to choose a slip from the hat. If he does not want the item, he passes the slip to heir #2, and on down the line. For the second item drawing, heir #2 draws first.

- Drunken Pin the Tail on the Donkey. My personal favorite. Have the heirs closely examine a board that has spaces listing the items. The heirs then do a line of shots, put on a blindfold, get spun around, and try to tag the item they want.

On the Web

- *Who Gets Grandma's Yellow Pie Plate? (A Guide to Passing on Personal Possessions)* by M. Stum.
  YellowPiePlate.UMN.edu/indexB.html

- *The Boomer Burden: Dealing with Your Parents' Lifetime Accumulation of Stuff* by Julie Hall.
  EstateLady.Wordpress.com

ORGANIZATION OF IMPORTANT PAPERS

As you go through this chapter, you may be astonished at the amount of documents you have and how unorganized you are. Do yourself and your loved ones a favor. Organize!

Below are some categories for you to consider when storing your documents:

- Immediate use—papers that you use weekly and monthly. These include current bills and receipts.

- Current use—papers you will use sometime during the calendar year. These files might include auto and health insurance policies, home maintenance contracts, deductible expense receipts, passports, and licenses.

- Infrequent use—papers you need to store for an indefinite term in case they are required for one reason or another. These papers might include warranties and guarantees, medical records, education records, bank statements, cancelled checks, and tax returns.

- Permanent files—these are papers you need to keep forever. These papers include anything that would be difficult or impossible to replace such as deeds, birth certificates, health records, titles of ownership, legal papers, contracts, life insurance policies, advance directives, and wills.

LOCATION OF IMPORTANT PAPERS

There are three basic places to keep your important papers:

- A filing cabinet, desk drawer, or cardboard box are good places for papers you use daily or monthly. These might include correspondence, forms, records, and bills.

- An in-home fireproof container is good for records not required on a daily basis but that are important. These might include certificates, wills, and CD or flash drive backups for your computer files.

- Safe deposit boxes are the best places to keep valuable papers. These papers might include negotiable instruments like stock certificates and bonds, a household inventory, jewelry appraisals, listings of insurance policies and credit card numbers, and a copy of your will.

TORONTO'S GREAT STORK DERBY

Upon his death in October of 1926, prankster and successful Ontario attorney Charles Vance Millar had his considerable wealth distributed in playful ways. He gave equal shares of a vacation home to three of his friends who were attorneys. The problem was, all three strongly disliked each other. He bequeathed shares in the Ontario Jockey Club to a judge and minister who reviled gambling. He gave shares of the O'Keefe Brewery Company to every Protestant minister and every Orange Lodge in Ontario, all of whom were strong proponents of prohibition. And finally, he gave the rest of his money to the Toronto woman who could produce the most children, certified by registrations under the Vital Statistics Act, in the 10-year period following the date of his death.

Read more about this man who had "his will his way": **Modern-Canadian-History.Suite101.com/article.cfm/charles_millar_lawyer_prankster**.

Computer Files

You need to leave instructions for your executor regarding your computer and the files on it. Perhaps have an icon titled "In case of my death" on your desktop that clicks through to a text file listing user names and passwords, e-mail addresses, and files to delete. Or put this text file on a flash drive and clearly mark the drive as to be read after your death. This text file likely should be password-protected. In this case, keep the password in your safe deposit box. Be sure to omit passwords for files your executor does not need to see (notes from your therapy sessions listing details of the plan you used to kill the neighbor's yapping dog).

Good to Know

- In its normal, helpful way, the IRS states on its web site: "Generally, you must keep your records that support an item of income or deductions on a tax return until the period of limitations for that return runs out." The IRS then goes on to list the many variables and time limits that run from two years to indefinitely. Visit the web site—**www.IRS.gov/businesses/small/article/0,,id=98513,00.html**—or check with your accountant, which is likely to be simpler.

- Organize your folders into groups, using labels such as: Insurance, Medical, House, Auto.

- Not to get all Martha Stewart on you, but using different colored folders for different types of information can be helpful.

On the Web

- ArticlesBase—An article titled "Easy Steps to an Organized Home Office". **ArticlesBase.com/home-business-articles/easy-steps-to-an-organized-home-office-164932.html**

- eHow—Information about how to arrange a home office. **EHow.com/how_13244_arrange-home-office.html**

- Legacy Locker—This web site will store web site member names and passwords, only allowing beneficiaries and heirs access when two verified family members, attorneys, or trusted friends confirm that you have indeed passed away. **LegacyLocker.com**

- Max About—An article with the great title "Arranging Your Drawers." **Articles.MaxAbout.com/artid0005782/arranging_your_drawers.aspx**

Death Certificate

Whoever is taking care of your business after you die will need to obtain a death certificate in order to do just about anything, including arranging for burial or cremation, probating your estate, settling your finances, and so forth. In the worksheet section in the back of the book is a list of information required for a death certificate for you to fill out. I know some of this information is repeated elsewhere, but remember, we are doing this to help the person who is left holding the bag—as it were.

The Ghost Trial of the Century

James Kidd was an Arizona copper miner who disappeared in November of 1946 after leaving on a prospecting trip near the legendary Lost Dutchman Gold Mine. When his will was finally read, he had left nearly a quarter of a million dollars to "research, or some scientific proof of a soul of the human body which leaves at death." At least 134 researchers and organizations filed a claim for the money and thus ensued what has been called "The Ghost Trial of the Century." **Answers.com/topic/james-kidd**

Death Benefits

A death benefit is money your survivors will get when you die. Hopefully, they will deserve it! (Just kidding.) This money can come from the government in the form of Social Security payments or other entitlements, from employment plans, insurance payouts, and more.

- These benefits will not just appear in your survivor's mailbox. They must be applied for, so it is critical that you record information about those payments to which you are entitled and provide this information to your executor.

- These benefits sometimes have time limitations for payout. When recording your death benefits, make a note of any time restrictions.

- The worksheet section has a list of different types of death benefits to get you started.

On the Web

- AFL-CIO survivor benefits: **AFLCIO.org/issues/safety/wc**.

- Federal employee survivor benefits: **FederalRetirement.net/survivor.htm**.

- Railroad retirement and survivor benefits: **RRB.gov/forms/opa/ib2/ib2_overview.asp**.

- State Survivor Benefits and Public Safety Officers' Benefits Program: **www.MyWayForward.com/government/survivor_benefits/state_survivor_benefits_and_public_safety_officers_benefits_program**.

- Social Security Administration: **www.SSA.gov/pubs/deathbenefits.htm**.

- Veterans Affairs Survivors and Dependents Benefits: **www.VBA.va.gov/survivors**.

SUDDEN DEATH CHECKLIST (*SEE THE WORKSHEETS IN THE BACK OF THE BOOK FOR MORE DETAILS*)

- With a sudden death at home, call 911. The paramedics will notify the police and the coroner.

- With an expected death at home, call your doctor. He will make the other calls.

- If the deceased has been under home-based hospice care, call the hospice organization.

- If the death occurred abroad, contact the Overseas Citizens Services Department of the U.S. Department of State: 1-888-407-4747 (from overseas: 202-501-4444); **Travel.State.gov/travel/tips/emergencies/emergencies_3878.html**.

CHAPTER 8

Here Comes the Sun: Attaining Closure from Grief

"When you are sorrowful look again in your heart, and you shall see that in truth you are weeping for that which has been your delight."
—Kahlil Gibran

Hard. Grief is hard. Anyone who has gone through it will tell you that. But they will also tell you that you can get through it. Helping your loved ones attain closure from the grief caused by your death is one of the most caring things you can do.

WHAT I KNOW IS TRUE

Having been there myself, let me share some things about grief that I know to be true:

- Grief is something that must be experienced. You cannot put it aside. You have to go through the process. If you try to shove it down, it can make you physically ill and damage your ability to have healthy relationships.

- Grief is complicated and deeply personal. Everyone will go through grief in their own way, in their own time, and with their own intensity.

- Grief washes over you like waves. Sometimes, the sea is calm and you get your feet on the bottom and then a wave knocks you down and you go under.

- One day you will wake up and grief will not be the first feeling you experience. But this takes its own, sweet time.

HELPING YOUR FRIENDS AND FAMILY

Here are some things you might want to consider doing for your family and friends to help them with their grieving process:

- Ask them to support a favorite cause in your memory or to plant a tree in your memory. See this obituary article about trees being planted in memory of Irish nationals and others at Muckross House in Killarney National Park to get the idea: **Obit-Mag.com/viewmedia.php/prmMID/4909**.

- The first holidays will be difficult for your friends and family. You might want to leave instructions asking them to put together a basket for the food bank in your memory, or make a Christmas ornament that has something to do with a memory of you, or dish out food at the homeless shelter.

- Leave instructions and funds for a gathering with good food and drink to be held on the first occasion of your birthday after your passing. Consider leaving a funny poem or a note containing a few special memories.

- Plan something special for select friends and family on the day of your service. I have an odd group of friends with a peculiar sense of humor. Each friend will receive instructions for "Burial Bingo." They will count how many times during the service and celebration they hear the following phrases: "It was God's will," "She's in a better place now," and "She would not want us to be sad." The friend with the most phrases receives a nice bottle of champagne.

- Leave a bag of eco-friendly balloons that friends can fill with helium and release into the sky on a date that was special to

you. Eco-friendly balloons can be found at Ecological Promos.
www.EcologicalPromos.com/2008/01/eco-friendly-product-of-week.html

- Ask family and friends to do something together on the first anniversary of your passing, such as a wine-tasting trip to Napa Valley, a picnic in your favorite park, or watching old home movies together.

- Leave a journal for each of your close friends and loved ones, especially children. Journaling can help one work through feelings. Memory and grief journals can be found at Memories Are Forever.
Memories-Are-Forever.org/memories/booksjournl-f.htm

- For the children who will be left behind, why not plan a special ceremony just for them? Perhaps they could draw pictures for you and then float the pictures out to sea to say goodbye.

- Pick out special items to leave to special people. Leave a note with each of these items, talking about a special memory tied to the item or saying how much the item and the recipient meant to you.

- Leave copies of a special picture for certain people, with a note about its significance to you.

- If you know when you are going to die, say from a terminal illness, you can plan to have your memorial party while you are still alive. It's been done before and people say it can be a wonderful event indeed. Read about the party for 300 that Julie Becker hosted before her death:
SeattlePI.com/lifestyle/311417_lifecelebrations13.html.

- This week, think of ten people who will deeply grieve your passing. Write each of them a note about how much they have meant to you. Try to include a memory or two and recall a funny incident if you can. Place these notes in the file with your will.

- For those special people whom you believe will have a hard time moving on, plan a small "releasing" ceremony to be held two months after your death. It can be a lovely, quiet way for loved ones to finally let you go. Items to include might be the eco-friendly balloons mentioned above or small paper boats to be sent out to sea.

- Give each a copy of the Grief Relief Resource list below.

Things You and Your Loved Ones Should Know About Grief

- Grief is a normal expression of loss that can be experienced in a physical, emotional, social, or religious manner. Everyone will grieve in his or her own way.

- Loved ones may experience the emotions of anger, denial, yearning, disbelief, guilt, confusion, sadness, humiliation, shock, and despair.

- Complicated grief is a response to loss that affects close relationships and belief systems, involves intense and unabated longing, and lasts for more than one year. When this is evident, it is time for professional help.

- An unexpected death can cause an increased risk of complicated grief, serious depression, or even post-traumatic stress disorder.

- Mourning is a good thing. It is the outward expression of your loss and can involve family and friends. Mourning with others and observing rituals can help make sense of a loved one's death.

- Grief triggers that remind you of a loss can appear without warning. Know that there are events or places that will sharply renew the feeling of loss, and be prepared for this to happen.

- There are basically seven stages of emotional grief. The stages do not have to be experienced in order but going through the process is helpful for closure and emotional health. The point is to come out whole on the other side. The stages are disbelief, denial, bargaining, guilt, anger, depression, and acceptance.

Spending time alone with your grief can be healing, but so can approaching others for comfort and help. *Photo courtesy of Images by Ruth (IslandPath.com)*

- The best thing grieving individuals can do for themselves is to eat nourishing food, begin to rebuild a normal schedule, get plenty of sleep, and talk to other caring individuals.

Grief Relief Resources

There are plenty of experts out there who are ready, willing, and able to share their wisdom and experience for those encountering grief. If you or someone you love are encountering deep grief, please consider making an appointment with an experienced, competent therapist or counselor.

Books

- *A Grief Observed* by C. S. Lewis (Harper One, 2001)

- *After the Darkest Hour: How Suffering Begins the Journey to Wisdom* by Kathleen A. Brehony, Ph.D. (Henry Holt & Company, 2001)

- *Good Life, Good Death* by Gehlek Rimpoche (Riverhead Trade, 2002)

- *The Grief Recovery Handbook, 20th Anniversary Expanded Edition: The Action Program for Moving Beyond Death, Divorce, and Other Losses including Health, Career, and Faith* by John W. James (Collins Living 2009)

- *Healing After Loss: Daily Meditations For Working Through Grief* by Martha W. Hickman (Collins Living, 1994)

- *I Wasn't Ready to Say Goodbye: Surviving, Coping and Healing After the Sudden Death of a Loved One* by Brook Noel and Pamela D. Blair (Sourcebooks Trade, 2008)

- *Midlife Orphan* by Jane Brooks (Berkley Trade; 1st edition, 1999)

- *On Death and Dying* by Elisabeth Kubler-Ross (Scribner, 1997)

- *On Grief and Grieving: Finding the Meaning of Grief Through the Five Stages of Loss* by Elisabeth Kubler-Ross and David Kessler (Scribner, 2005)

- *Swallowed By A Snake: The Gift of the Masculine Side of Healing* by Thomas R. Golden (Golden Healing Publishing, 1996)

- *Using the Power of Hope to Cope with Dying: The Four Stages of Hope* by Cathleen Fanslow-Brunjes, M.A., R.N. (Quill Driver Books, 2008)

- *When Children Grieve: For Adults to Help Children Deal with Death, Divorce, Pet Loss, Moving, and Other Losses* by John W. James ("Grief Recovery Handbook" Collins Living, 2002)

- *The Year of Magical Thinking* by Joan Didion (Knopf, 2005)

Websites

- AARP—An article listing the seven choices of grief: **AARP.org/family/lifeafterloss/articles/seven_choices_of_ grief.html**

- Elisabeth Kubler Ross—Official website: **ElisabethKublerRoss.com**

- GriefNet—An Internet community of persons dealing with grief, death, and major loss: **GriefNet.org**

- GriefShare—Grief support recovery groups: **GriefShare.org**

- Harvard Medical School—An article on complicated grief: **www.health.harvard.edu/fhg/updates/Complicated-grief. shtml**

- Idea Marketers—An article titled "The First Christmas After a Death" by Susan Dunn: **IdeaMarketers.com/?articleid=35094**

- Journey of Hearts—An online place for anyone grieving a loss: **JourneyOfHearts.org**

- Mayo Clinic—An article on complicated grief:
  MayoClinic.com/print/complicated-grief/DS01023/

- Recover-From-Grief—A site for grief loss recovery, hope, and
  health through creative grieving: **Recover-From-Grief.com**

- Slate.com—"The Long Goodbye: A Study of Bereavement" by
  Meghan O'Rourke. An excellent series on grieving.
  Slate.com/id/2211257/entry/2211256

Organizations

- The Air Crash Support Network—The ACSN is a national
  non-political, nonprofit, tax-exempt organization established to
  aid and facilitate the grieving process of people who have been
  affected by or involved in an air crash. **AccessHelp.org**

- Compassionate Friends—This is a self-help organization whose
  purpose is to offer friendship and understanding to parents and
  siblings following the death of a child.
  CompassionateFriends.org

- The Dougy Center for Grieving Children and Families—The
  Dougy Center provides age-specific support groups for grieving children (3–5, 6–12, teens), and loss-specific groups as well
  (parent death, sibling death, survivors of homicide/violent
  death, survivors of suicide). **Dougy.org**

- Grief Support Services.Org—A Program of national grief support services database.
  GriefSupportServices.org/newgrief/index.php

- International Association of Fire Fighters—The IAFF provides
  its 250,000 members, who are firefighters and paramedics, with
  services such as employee assistance and trauma counseling in
  the event of a line-of-duty death. **IAFF.org**

- Lifekeeper Memory Quilts—The Suicide Prevention Action
  Network SPAN USA's Quilt Organizers help coordinate and

create Lifekeeper Memory Quilts. Currently there are about 100 quilts in 43 different states. **SpanUSA.org**

- The National Center for Jewish Healing—The NCJH helps communities better meet the spiritual needs of Jews living with illness, loss, and other significant life challenges. **NCJH.org**

- Parents Of Murdered Children, Inc.—PMOC provides support and assistance to all survivors of homicide victims. **POMC.com**

- Tragedy Assistance Program for Survivors—TAPS is a national non-profit organization made up of, and providing services at no cost to, all those who have suffered the loss of a loved one in the armed forces. **TAPS.org**

- Widowed Persons Service—An AARP organization for newly widowed persons. **Seniors-Site.com/widowm/wps.html**

Appendix 1

The *Death for Beginners* Worksheets

Introduction to the Worksheets

The following worksheets are designed to do two things:

- Help you think through the many choices you may wish to make concerning your final journey and beyond.

- Provide written instructions for you to give to the person or people who will be handling your affairs after you die.

As you move through the worksheets, make a check mark in the appropriate boxes and record necessary information in the blanks. In places where the details you wish to provide will not fit in the space provided, add additional pages as needed and note this on the worksheet. Important note:

Instructions for filling out the worksheets appear in italics typeface.

You'll be guided to skip unnecessary parts of the worksheets, depending on the choices you make. Feel free to leave blank those sections where you're ok with having someone else makes the decision, or those areas you don't yet have information for. You can always update your worksheets later.

As you work through them, the worksheets will refer you to appropriate chapters of the book so you can refresh your memory on the details of the various choices when needed. After you finish filling out the worksheets and any additional pages, simply make photocopies to hand out. Be sure to keep a copy for yourself. When you update the worksheets, make new photocopies and hand them out again. You can always print out clean blank copies of the worksheets at **www.DeathForBeginners.com**.

My Choices Worksheet

The following worksheet records my wishes in the event of my death. Thank you in advance for adhering to them as closely as possible. I've left blank the areas that I don't have any strong feelings about. Please make decisions that you think best in those areas.

Name:

_____

Today's date:

_____

Financial information, insurance policies, required permits and applications, an eulogy or obituary if I have written one, additional pages and other relevant paperwork is:

☐ Attached

☐ Located here:

_____

The location of my will, which names my executor, is:

_____

_____

_____

What I Want Done With My Body

Choose one of the six options below and provide the appropriate information. Refer to Chapter One for clarification when necessary.

☐ Option 1: I would like to bequeath my body to a medical school (see page 2)

Medical school name and contact information:

_____

_____

_____

☐ I do not wish for my remains to be returned. (*Skip to the "Memorial Marker with No Gravesite" section on page 179*).

☐ I would like my remains to be returned.

Choose one of the two options below:

　　☐ I would like my remains to be buried. (*Skip to the "I Wish to Be Buried" section on page 163.*)

　　☐ I would like my remains to be cremated. (*Skip to the "I Wish to Be Cremated" section on page 169.*)

If the school declines the donation, my alternate choice is:

☐ Bequeath my body to a body farm

☐ Traditional care

☐ Direct disposition

☐ Self-service

☐ Cryonics

☐ No preference

☐ Option 2: I would like to bequeath my body to a body farm (see page 2)

Forensic anthropology center name and contact information:

_____

_____

If the farm declines the donation, my alternate choice is:

☐ Bequeath my body to a medical school

☐ Traditional care

☐ Direct disposition

☐ Self-service

☐ Cryonics

☐ No preference

☐ Option 3: I would like my body to be dealt with traditionally (see page 13)

Name of funeral home and contact information:

_____

_____

With this choice, select one of the following options:

☐ I would like my remains to be buried. (*Skip to the "I Wish to Be Buried" section on page 163.*)

☐ I would like my remains to be cremated. (*Skip to the "I Wish to be Cremated" section on page 169.*)

☐ Option 4: I would like direct disposition of my body (see page 9)

Name of funeral service:

_____

_____

_____

With this choice, select one of the following options:

☐ I would like my remains to be buried. (*Skip to the "I Wish to Be Buried" section on page 163.*)

☐ I would like my remains to be cremated. (*Skip to the "I Wish to Be Cremated" section on page 169.*)

☐ Option 5: I would prefer self-service (see page 11)

Name and contact information for person who will be in charge:

_____

_____

_____

With this choice, select one of the following options:

☐ I would like my remains to be buried. (*Skip to the "I Wish to Be Buried" section on page 163.*)

☐ I would like my remains to be cremated. (*Skip to the "I Wish to Be Cremated" section on page 169.*)

☐ **Option 6: I would like to preserve my body via cryonics (see page 14)**

Name and contact information of cryonic organization:

_____

_____

_____

If you chose cryonics, skip to the "Memorial Marker with no Gravesite" section on page 179.

☐ I Wish to Be Buried

Check the box above if you wish to be buried. You have four choices for burial. Choose one of the options and provide the appropriate information. Refer to Chapter Two for clarification when necessary. If you would rather be cremated, skip to the "I Wish to Be Cremated" section on page 169.)

☐ Option 1: I wish to have a traditional burial (see page 21)

Name of funeral home and contact information:

_____

_____

_____

☐ I wish to be embalmed (see page 31)

OR

☐ I prefer refrigeration without embalming

Choose one of the following two options for where you want to be buried:

☐ I prefer burial in the Earth (see page 23)

    ☐ use a vault

    ☐ use a liner

    ☐ use neither

    ☐ in a plot

    ☐ in a grave

    OR

☐ I prefer entombment (see page 25)

    ☐ in an above ground mausoleum

    ☐ in an underground crypt

Name, location, and contact information of cemetery or mausoleum:

_____

_____

_____

    ☐ I am a veteran and wish to be buried in a national cemetery (see page 26).

If you chose a Traditional Burial, skip to the "My Casket Choices" section on page 167.

☐ Option 2: I wish to have a green or natural burial (see page 28)

Choose from one of the following types of cemeteries:

☐ I prefer a conventional cemetery.

☐ I prefer a natural burial ground.

☐ I prefer a conservation burial ground.

Name, location and contact information of cemetery:

_____

_____

_____

If you chose a green or natural burial, skip to the "My Casket Choices" section on page 167.

☐ Option 3: I wish to be buried at sea (see page 33)

Name and contact information of maritime funeral director:

_____

_____

_____

Location of commitment:

_____

_____

_____

☐ I am a veteran and wish to be buried at sea by the United States Navy (see page 36).

I would prefer the following be used for my body:

☐ sailcloth

☐ a weighted body bag

☐ a marine coffin

☐ no preference

If you chose to be buried at sea, skip to the "Memorial Marker with No Gravesite" section on page 179.

☐ Option 4: I wish to have a home burial or other non-cemetery site (see page 38)

Location of burial site:

_____

_____

_____

Name and contact information of person or company to provide necessary services:

_____

_____

_____

Necessary permits have been acquired and are attached to this worksheet?

☐ yes

☐ no

If you chose a home burial, move to the "My Casket Choices" section on the next page.

My Four Casket Choices

Choose one of the four options below and provide the appropriate information. Refer to Chapter One for clarification when necessary.

☐ **I wish to have a traditional casket (see page 66).**

☐ **I wish to have a nontraditional casket (see page 69).**

☐ **I wish to have a green or natural casket (see page 72).**

☐ **I wish to have a homemade casket. (see page 74).**

☐ **I have checked with the cemetery and they have approved this type of casket.**

Details:

_____

_____

_____

☐ I have already purchased my casket. Here are the details, including the location:

_____

_____

_____

☐ I have picked out a casket, but haven't purchased it; here are the details:

_____

_____

_____

☐ I have not picked out my casket but I want to spend only this amount of money: $_____.

Skip to the "I Wish to Have a Memorial Marker" section on page 177.

IF I DIE OUTSIDE OF THE COUNTRY:

☐ **Ship the entire body home.**

☐ **Cremate my remains and then ship the remains home.**

☐ I WISH TO BE CREMATED

Check the box above if you wish to be cremated. Choose from the following options and provide the appropriate information. Refer to Chapter Three for clarification when necessary.

☐ I want direct cremation (see page 50).

OR

☐ I want a traditional cremation (see page 51).

Name and contact information of crematorium:

_____

_____

_____

☐ I wish to have a funeral service handle the transportation of my body.

Name and contact information of funeral service provider:

_____

_____

_____

OR

☐ **I wish to not use a funeral service.**

Person in charge of transporting body if no funeral service provider is used:

_____

_____

_____

☐ **I wish to be embalmed.**

OR

☐ **I prefer refrigeration without embalming.**

My Four Pre-Cremation Coffin Choices

☐ **I wish to have a traditional crematorium-approved coffin (see page 77).**

☐ **I prefer to have a rental coffin to be used for the service or viewing (see page 78).**

☐ **I prefer an inexpensive crematorium-provided container not suitable for use at a service or a viewing (see page 78).**

☐ **I wish to have a nontraditional casket (see page 79):**

☐ I wish to have a green or natural casket.

☐ I wish to have a homemade casket.

☐ I have checked with the crematorium and they have approved this type of casket.

Details:

_____

_____

_____

☐ I have already purchased my casket. Here are the details, including the location:

_____

_____

_____

☐ I have picked out a casket, but haven't purchased it; here are the details:

_____

_____

_____

☐ I have not picked out my casket but I want to spend only this amount of money: $_____.

Continue to the following section, "My Urn Choices."

My Four Urn Choices

☐ **I wish to have a traditional urn (see page 80).**

☐ **I wish to have a nontraditional urn (see page 82).**

> ☐ I wish to have a green, natural, or homemade urn. Here are the details:

_____

_____

_____

☐ **A crematorium-provided urn is fine with me (see page 84).**

☐ **I wish to have an urn that is made for scattering ashes (see page 82).**

☐ **I have already purchased my urn; here are the details:**

_____

_____

_____

☐ **I have picked out a urn, but haven't purchased it, here are the details:**

_____

_____

_____

☐ **I have not picked out my casket but I want to spend only this amount of money: $_____.**

What I Want Done with My Ashes (see pages 55–60)

Choose one of the eight options below and provide the appropriate information. Refer to Chapter Three for clarification when necessary.

☐ **Option 1: I would like my ashes buried in a cemetery (see page 55).**

  ☐ I am a veteran and wish for my ashes to be buried in a national cemetery.

☐ **Option 2: I would like the urn my ashes are in to be placed in a columbarium (see page 57).**

Name, location and contact information of cemetery or columbarium:

_____

_____

_____

☐ **Option 3: I wish to have my ashes buried at home or at another non-cemetery site (see page 58).**

Name and location of burial site:

_____

_____

_____

Persons I would like to be in charge of this:

_____

_____

☐ **Option 4: I wish for my ashes to be buried at sea (see page 56).**

Name and contact information of maritime funeral director:

_____

☐ I am a veteran and wish for my ashes to be buried at sea by the United States Navy (see page 56).

☐ **Option 5: I would like the urn my ashes are in to be placed in a home or other private setting (see page 58).**

Location:

_____

_____

_____

Persons I would like to be in charge of this:

_____

_____

☐ Option 6: I would like my ashes scattered (see page 58).

☐ by hand

☐ by balloon

☐ by potato gun

☐ other: _____

Location for my ashes to be scattered:

_____

_____

_____

Persons I would like to be in charge of this:

_____

_____

Permits, if any are required, have been acquired and are attached to this worksheet:

☐ Yes

☐ No

☐ **Option 7: I would like some or all of my ashes to be made into (see page 59).**

☐ an ocean reef

☐ a piece of jewelry

☐ a walking stick

☐ potting soil

☐ other: _____

Name and contact information of the company or organization that be in charge of doing this:

_____

_____

_____

If you choose to have only some of your ashes made into an object, be sure to make another selection detailing what you want done with the remainder of your ashes.

☐ **Option 8: I have my own ideas about what I want done with my ashes. Here are the details:**

_____

_____

_____

☐ I *DO NOT* WISH TO HAVE A MEMORIAL MARKER.

Skip to the "I Want a Service or Celebration" section on page 179 if you do not wish to have a memorial marker, otherwise continue below. Refer to Chapter Six for clarification when necessary.

☐ I WISH TO HAVE A MEMORIAL MARKER (SEE PAGES 121–125).

☐ I have already purchased my marker. Here are the details, including its location:

_____

_____

_____

☐ I have cemetery approval for this marker.

☐ I have picked out a marker, but haven't purchased it. Here are the details:

_____

_____

_____

☐ I have cemetery approval for this marker.

☐ **I have not picked out a marker, but I want to spend only this amount of money: $_____.**

☐ **I am a veteran and the Department of Veterans Affairs will furnish a government headstone or marker (see page 122).**

☐ **I would like my marker made from the following materials:**

_____

_____

☐ **I would like my marker to look like the following:**

_____

_____

☐ **I would like the following words to appear on my marker:**

_____

_____

_____

☐ **Since I won't have a gravesite (as is the case with a burial at sea, a scattering of ashes, and similar methods of the disposal of remains (see page 126)), I would like my marker to be placed as follows:**

Location and pertinent details:

_____

_____

_____

☐ **I *Do not* Want a Service or Celebration.**

If you wish for there to be a service or a celebration of your life, complete the appropriate sections below. If you don't want either, skip this section and continue to "I Want an Eulogy" on page 186. Refer to Chapter Five for clarification when necessary.

☐ **I Want a Service or Celebration.**

☐ **I would like the following (see pages 92–98):**

☐ a traditional funeral

☐ a memorial service

☐ a committal service

☐ an alternative service

☐ **I would like the format to be (see pages 98–102):**

☐ religious

☐ nonreligious

☐ private

☐ a family gathering

☐ wild and crazy

Location:

_____

_____

_____

Person I would like to preside:

_____

_____

_____

Additional speakers should include

_____

_____

_____

☐ I would like the following readings and remembrances to be
  presented:

_____

_____

☐ I would like the following music to be played, organist to play, soloist to sing:

_____

_____

_____

☐ I would like a video presentation.

Person or persons I would like to be in charge of this:

_____

_____

_____

☐ I would like printed programs to include the following verses, pictures, photographs, biography, eulogy:

_____

_____

_____

_____

181

☐ I would like these items on my memorial table:

_____

_____

_____

☐ I would like my casket or urn to be present.

    ☐ I would like the casket open.

    ☐ I would like the casket closed.

☐ I would like the following people to be pallbearers and honorary pallbearers:

_____

_____

_____

☐ I don't want my casket or urn to be present.

☐ Things I specifically do *not* want included in my service:

_____

_____

_____

☐ Additional things I would like including flowers and special decorations:

_____

_____

_____

☐ I Do *Not* Want a Wake.

Skip to the next section if you don't wish to have a wake or don't care one way or another.

☐ I Would Like a Wake (SEE PAGE 107).

☐ I would like my casket or urn to be at the wake.

☐ I don't want my casket or urn to be at the wake.

Location and other details including memorial table items, music, special stories, food, a toast, a message to be read and a gift to the owner if applicable.

_____

_____

_____

_____

_____

Person or persons I would like to be in charge of this:

_____

_____

_____

☐ **I Do *Not* Want a Visitation.**

Skip to the next section if you don't wish to have a visitation or don't care one way or another.

☐ **I Would Like a Visitation (see page 105).**

☐ **I would like my visitation to be formal.**

☐ **I would like my visitation to be informal.**

Location and other details including video presentation, readings, memorial table items, music, flowers, food, drink, and information for printed programs:

_____

_____

_____

Person or persons I would like to be in charge of this:

_____

_____

_____

□ **I would like a small service included in my visitation.**

Location and other details including readings, video, music, flowers, speakers and printed programs:

_____

_____

_____

Person or persons I would like to be in charge of this:

_____

_____

□ **I Do *Not* Want a Viewing.**

Skip to the next section if you don't wish to have a viewing or don't care one way or another.

□ **I Would Like a Viewing (see page 105).**

□ **I would like my viewing to be formal.**

□ **I would like my viewing to be informal.**

Location and other details including instructions about makeup and hair, photograph for mortician, clothing, jewelry and what should be done with your jewelry afterwards, video, items for memorial table, if any, flowers and music:

_____

_____

_____

_____

Person or persons I would like to be in charge of this:

_____

_____

☐ I Do *Not* Want a Eulogy.

Skip to the next section if you don't wish to have a eulogy or don't care one way or another.

☐ I Would Like a Eulogy (see page 103).

☐ I have written my eulogy and it is:

☐ attached

☐ located here: _____

☐ I would like the following person to write my eulogy:

_____

☐ I would like my eulogy to contain the following information including theme, accomplishments, what was important to me and how my life reflected it, specific readings or quotes, anecdotes, dreams and wishes for those left behind:

_____

_____

_____

_____

_____

☐ I would like the following omitted from my eulogy:

_____

_____

_____

☐ I would like the following person to read my eulogy:

_____

☐ **BURIAL OR SCATTERING AFTER SERVICE**

☐ I would like a burial or scattering of ashes directly following the service.

Location and other details including music, readings and person to preside.

_____

_____

_____

OR

☐ **I would like a burial or scattering of ashes to be held at a later date.**

Location and other details including whether it will be private, open to only a few friends or open to all, if there will be a small service, music, readings, person to preside.

_____

_____

_____

☐ **I Do *Not* Want a Reception.**

Skip to the next section if you don't wish to have a reception or don't care one way or another.

☐ **I Would Like a Reception (see pages 108–111).**

☐ **I would like my reception to be formal.**

☐ I would like my reception to be informal.

Location and other details including music, flowers, personal message to be read, special stories to be recounted, memorial table items, food, drink, video, special decorations or displays, as well as anything I specifically do not want at the reception:

_____

_____

_____

_____

_____

Person or persons I would like to be in charge of this:

_____

_____

☐ I Do *Not* Want an Obituary.

Skip to the next section if you don't wish to have an obituary or don't care one way or another.

☐ I Would Like an Obituary (see pages 114–118).

You will list information for your obituary in the Personal Information section on page 194.

☐ I have written my obituary and it is:

☐ attached

☐ located here: _____

☐ **Include the photo that is:**

☐ attached

☐ located here: _____

☐ **Include the following donation in lieu of flowers:**

_____

_____

☐ **I want the following person to write my obituary:**

_____

☐ **I do *not* want the following mentioned in my obituary:**

_____

_____

☐ **I do *not* want the following person or persons to write my obituary:**

_____

_____

☐ I would like my obituary to:

☐ Be sent to these newspapers:

_____

_____

☐ Posted on these social or business websites:

_____

☐ Sent to these organizations (social and professional):

_____

☐ Sent to these professional magazines:

_____

☐ I would a special memorial posted at these sites (see page 125):

_____

_____

☐ I would like my on-line memorial page to include the following (e.g. biography, video, audio, pictures, donation button, links, guestbook):

_____

_____

_____

☐ **I DO *NOT* WANT TO DONATE MY ORGANS.**

Skip to the next section if you don't wish to donate your organs or don't care one way or another.

☐ **I WOULD LIKE TO DONATE MY ORGANS (SEE PAGE 6).**

  ☐ **I wish to donate everything that can be used.**

  ☐ **I wish to donate only the following circled items:**

Organs : Heart, lungs, kidneys, pancreas, liver, intestines;

Tissues: Corneas, skin, veins, tendons, bone, bone marrow, heart valves, connective tissue, the middle ear, cartilage, ligaments;

Stem Cells: Marrow, peripheral blood stem cells, cord blood stem cells; Blood products: Blood, platelets:

Other instructions include:

_____

_____

_____

☐ A uniform donor card has been filled out and is attached to this worksheet:

☐ Yes

☐ No

See below for the uniform donor card.

UNIFORM DONOR CARD

I, _____, have spoken to my family about organ and tissue donation. The following people have witnessed my commitment to be a donor.

I wish to donate the following:

☐ any needed organs and tissue,

☐ only the following organs and tissue:

_____

_____

_____

Donor Signature:_____ Date:_____

Witness:_____

Witness:_____

Next of Kin:_____

Telephone:(___)_____

PERSONAL INFORMATION

MY PERSONAL INFORMATION

Please use this information for my obituary, if any, the death certificate, and for other legal or benefits requirements. I have attached additional pages where needed.

Full name (including maiden name, if appropriate):

_____

Current address:

_____

_____

Phone:

_____

Date of birth:

_____

Place of birth:

_____

Social Security Number:

_____

Name of my Spouse or partner:

_____

My children and their spouses or partners:

_____

_____

My grandchildren:

_____

_____

Full name of both mother and father:

_____

_____

My siblings:

_____

_____

_____

My other relatives' names and relationships:

_____

_____

_____

_____

_____

My other special friends, pets and associates:

_____

_____

_____

My education:

_____

_____

My designations, awards, achievements, and other recognition:

_____

_____

_____

_____

My employment:

_____

_____

_____

_____

My hobbies, sports and other activities including volunteering:

_____

_____

My affiliations (including local and national professional, religious, and political organizations:

_____

_____

_____

Places I've lived:

_____

_____

_____

☐ **I am a veteran.**

Service serial number

_____

Service branch

_____

Dates of service and discharge rank

_____

Medals of special service

_____

PEOPLE TO BE NOTIFIED

Please notify these friends and family immediately:

Name:

_____

Phone:

_____

Name:

_____

Phone:

_____

Name:

_____

Phone:

_____

Name:

_____

Phone:

_____

Name:

_____

Phone:

_____

Name:

_____

Phone:

_____

Please notify these people immediately:

Attorney or legal advisor:

_____

Phone:

_____

Accountant or financial advisor:

_____

Phone:

_____

Executor of my estate:

_____

Phone:

_____

Physician:

_____

Phone:

_____

Spiritual Counselor:

_____

Phone:

_____

PAPERS TO BE GATHERED IMMEDIATELY

Checkmark if you have these items and papers and include their location.

☐ **Safe Deposit Box, including name on account, institution, box number, key location and assignee:**

_____

☐ **Will:**

_____

☐ **Durable Power of Attorney:**

_____

☐ **Computer information, USB stick, passwords:**

_____

☐ **Checkbook:**

_____

☐ **Current bills:**

_____

☐ **Birth certificate:**

_____

OTHER PAPERS THAT WILL BE NEEDED LATER

Checkmark if you have these items and papers and include their location.

☐ **Certificates of marriage, baptism:**

_____

☐ **Legal papers including divorce, nationalization, adoption:**

_____

☐ **Non-financial contracts:**

_____

DEATH BENEFITS INFORMATION

Check if you have these benefits and provide the company name, contact information, policy number, amount, and beneficiary.

☐ **Annuities:**

_____

_____

☐ **Pensions:**

_____

_____

☐ **Employer profit-sharing / 401K:**

_____

_____

☐ **Employer workman's compensation (supplemental to insurance):**

_____

_____

☐ **Medicare:**

_____

_____

☐ **Veterans Administration:**

_____

_____

☐ **Social Security:**

_____

_____

☐ **Memorial society or pre-paid funeral plans:**

_____

_____

☐ **Mutual aid plans such as church groups::**

_____

_____

☐ **Federal, state, or local employees' benefit programs:**

_____

_____

INSURANCE INFORMATION

Check if you have these benefits and provide the company name, contact information, policy number, amount, and beneficiary.

☐ **Life insurance:**

_____

_____

☐ **Medical insurance:**

_____

_____

☐ **Veterans' insurance:**

_____

_____

☐ **Annuities insurance:**

_____

_____

☐ **Pension insurance:**

_____

_____

☐ **Health and accident insurance:**

_____

_____

☐ Auto and Casualty insurance:

_____

_____

☐ State or governmental compensation insurance:

_____

_____

☐ Fraternal, Trade, Credit Union insurance:

_____

_____

☐ Employer accident insurance:

_____

_____

☐ Federal Government Railroad Retirement Board insurance:

_____

_____

FINANCIAL INFORMATION

Check if you have these financial holdings and provide the institution, name on account, and account number.

☐ **Checking account:**

_____

_____

☐ **Savings account:**

_____

_____

☐ **IRA:**

_____

_____

☐ **CD:**

_____

_____

☐ **Money market:**

_____

_____

☐ **Stocks and bonds:**

_____

_____

☐ **Credit cards:**

_____

_____

☐ **Mortgages:**

_____

_____

☐ **Promissory notes:**

_____

_____

REAL ESTATE INFORMATION

Check if you have these holdings and provide the location, deed holder, date acquired, and purchase price.

☐ **House, condominium, co-op:**

_____

_____

☐ **Out-of-state property:**

_____

_____

☐ **Rental Property:**

_____

_____

OTHER TITLES, DEEDS AND LEASES

Check if you have these holdings and provide the proper information including make, year, model, and license number.

☐ **Automobile:**

_____

_____

☐ **Boat:**

_____

_____

☐ **RV:**

_____

_____

☐ **Other:**

_____

_____

SUDDEN DEATH CHECKLIST

If you have to attend to the death of another, this checklist will be helpful.

IF YOU ARE PRESENT AT TIME OF DEATH:

☐ Sudden death at home, call 911. The paramedics will notify police and coroner.

☐ Expected death at home, call your doctor. He will make the other calls.

☐ Expected death at home with hospice care, call the hospice organization.

☐ Death abroad, contact the Overseas Citizens Services Department of the U.S. Department of State: 1-888-407-4747 (from overseas: 202-501-4444) **travel.state.gov/travel/tips/emergencies/emergencies_3878.html**.

IMMEDIATE DECISIONS/ACTIONS

☐ Autopsy—Usually required for unattended death or death at home, depending on the decision of the medical examiner. If an autopsy is not required but you want one, you may have to pay a fee that can range up to several thousand dollars. It usually takes two months for the full results of an autopsy to become available.

☐ Organ Donation—Do you know the deceased's wishes? Look for a donor card. Let hospital staff know immediately. Organs must be used between 6 and 72 hours after removal from the donor's body. One can donate heart, lungs, kidneys, pancreas, liver, intestines, corneas, skin, veins, tendons, bone, bone marrow, heart valves, connective tissue, and blood.

☐ Dependents— Check on dependents needing immediate care. This may include children, the disabled and elderly dependents. Don't forget all pets.

☐ Disposition of Body— If no instructions have been left, ask the deceased's family, spiritual guidance provider or legal advisor. For options, see Chapter One.

Immediate Notifications by Phone

☐ Immediate family and close friends

☐ Doctor, if not already called

☐ Priest, minister, family counselor, rabbi, or other spiritual advisor

☐ Executor of estate

☐ Attorney

☐ A friend to brainstorm with

☐ Any relative who will have to make travel plans

☐ Employer

☐ Funeral provider

Secondary Phone Notifications

☐ Extended family

☐ Extended circle of friends

☐ Neighbors

☐ Children's teachers

SECONDARY DECISIONS/ACTIONS

- ☐ Find the will and give it to the executor
- ☐ Gather all deceased's vital statistics for the death certificate
- ☐ Get at least 10 certified copies of the death certificate
- ☐ Look for bills, credit cards, mortgages, things needing immediate payment
- ☐ Cancel subscriptions to newspaper, internet, TV accounts, magazines, etc.
- ☐ Notify all utilities and have mail forwarded
- ☐ Arrange for house sitting, if needed
- ☐ Write the obituary—see Chapter 6 for suggestions
- ☐ Have someone start on the eulogy—see Chapter 5 for suggestions
- ☐ Start planning the service / funeral / interment —see Chapter 5 for suggestions

THIRD ROUND OF NOTIFICATIONS

- ☐ Phone calls to standing appointments such as hairdresser, volunteer committee, social clubs
- ☐ Phone calls to therapists, other doctors, house and garden help.
- ☐ Formal e-mail sent to distant family members, casual friends, selected business associates, and membership programs such as gyms, library, and recreation centers
- ☐ Written formal notice sent to business clients, professional licenses such as medical licenses, bar associations, CPA associations.

OTHER DECISIONS

- ☐ Look back at the worksheets for ideas regarding all arrangements.
- ☐ Have someone coordinate hospitality and transportation for out of town visitors.
- ☐ Choose someone to send acknowledgements after the fact as a thank you.
- ☐ Coordinate who supplies the food for the next couple of days.
- ☐ Decide where funeral flowers will be sent afterwards.
- ☐ Choose someone to take turns answering door, recording calls and gifts.
- ☐ Check to see if the house needs to be cleaned etc.
- ☐ Have someone stay at the residence during the funeral.
- ☐ Have a computer savvy friend place announcements on social networking sites.
- ☐ Arrange for transportation for the day of the funeral.
- ☐ Make arrangements for child care during service and reception.
- ☐ Arrange for any gratuities that will be necessary.

DAY OF FUNERAL

- ☐ Someone responsible specifically for getting everyone dressed and out of the door.
- ☐ Have someone in charge at the home, phones, and coordination on the day of the funeral.
- ☐ Have someone house sit during services.

☐ EHow—"How To Plan A Funeral":
www.EHow.com/how_3455_funeral.html

☐ "How to Plan an Affordable Funeral," Kimberly Palmer, October 17, 2007, *U.S. News & World Report:*
www.USNews.com/blogs/alpha-consumer/2007/10/17/ how-to-plan-an-affordable-funeral.html

PHONE NUMBERS YOU MAY NEED

☐ Social Security: 1-800-772-1213 (TTY) 1-800-325-0778.

☐ Medicare: 1-800-MEDICARE (1-800-633-4227).

☐ Veterans Affairs: 1-800-827-1000 (TDD) 1-800-829-4833.

☐ Veteran Affairs, retired and receiving military retired pay: call the Defense Finance and Accounting Service (DFAS), at 1-800-321-1080.

☐ Veteran Affairs, retired and receiving compensation or pension from the VA: 800-827-1000.

☐ Active Military:

    ☐ Air Force: 877-353-6807

    ☐ Army: 800 626-3317

    ☐ Navy: 800-368-3202

    ☐ Marines: 800-847-1597

    ☐ Coast Guard: 800-323-7233

☐ Credit reporting agencies:

    ☐ Equifax: 1-888-766-0008

    ☐ TransUnion: 1-888-909-8872

    ☐ Experian: 1-888-397-3742

☐ Department of Motor Vehicles

☐ Internal Revenue Service 1-800-829-1040 (TDD)1-800-829-4059.

You have completed the worksheets!

Feel free to make extra notes and attach them to this document. Now is the time to make copies and distribute them to those who you believe will be left behind to take care of business.

*You can always download fresh versions of the worksheets at **DeathForBeginners.com**. I urge you to consider telling your friends and family to download the forms for their own use—just be sure to let them know that everything in the worksheets makes much more sense if they buy the* Death For Beginners *book, as well.*

Congratulations! You have done a very good thing.

Happy Trails!

—Karen Jones

APPENDIX 2

General Resources

BOOKS

Bondesen, Jan. *Buried Alive: The Terrifying History of Our Most Primal Fear*. New York: W. W. Norton , 2001.

Consumers Union. *Funerals: Consumer's Last Rights*. Mount Vernon, NY: Consumers Union, 1977.

Davies, Rodney. *The Lazarus Syndrome: Burial Alive and Other Horrors of the Undead*. New York: Barnes and Noble, 1998.

Ford, Josephine M. *The Silver Lining: Personalized Scriptural Wake Services*. Mystic, CT: Twenty Third Publications, 1987.

Lamm, Maurice. *The Jewish Way of Death and Mourning*. NY: Jonathan David, 1969.

Lamont, Corliss. *A Humanist Funeral Service*. Buffalo, NY: Prometheus Books, 1977.

Langford, E. *Planning a Christian Funeral*. NY: Disciple Resources, 1989.

Miller, William. *The Funeral Book: An Insiders Advice for Saving Money and Reducing Stress*. NY: Robert D. Reed, 1994.

Mitford, Jessica: *The American Way of Death Revisited*. Knopf, Rev Sub edition, 1998.

Morgan, Earnest. *Dealing Creatively with Death: A Manual of Death Education and Simple Burial*. Burnsville, NC: Cleo Press, 1990.

Quaker Home Service, Funerals And Memorial Meetings. London. Quaker Books; Rev Ed edition (December 2003).

Wilson, Jane Wynne. *Funerals Without God: A Practical Guide to Non-Religious Funerals*. Buffalo, NY: Prometheus Books, 1990.

Young, Gregory W. The *High Cost of Dying*. Amherst, NY: Prometheus Books, 1994.

ORGANIZATIONS

The American Association of Tissue Banks
Includes more than 100 accredited tissue banks, 1,100 individual members. More than 30,000 donors provide more than 1.5 million tissue grafts annually for transplant in the United States. **AATB.org**

1320 Old Chain Bridge Road, Suite 450, McLean, VA 22101

Phone: 703-827-9582 | Fax: 703-356-2198 | E-mail: aatb@aatb.org

American Humanist Association
Provides information about Humanistic funeral services.

1777 T Street, NW, Washington, DC 20009-7125

Phone: 202-238-9088 / Toll free: 800-837-3792

Fax: 202-238-9003

AmericanHumanist.org

The Better Business Bureau
BBB.org/us/

Eye Bank Association of America
A not-for-profit organization of eye banks dedicated to the restoration of sight through the promotion and advancement of eye banking.

1015 Eighteenth Street NW, Suite 1010, Washington, DC 20036

Phone: 202-775-4999 / Fax: 202-429-6036

RestoreSight.org

Funeral Consumers Alliance
A nonprofit organization dedicated to protecting a consumer's right to choose a meaningful, dignified, affordable funeral.

33 Patchen Road, South Burlington, VT 05403

Toll-free: 800-765-0107

fca@funerals.org   **Funerals.org**

International Cemetery, Cremation & Funeral Association
107 Carpenter Dr, Suite 100, Sterling, VA 20164

Phone: 703-391-8400 / TollFree 800-645-7700 / Fax 703-391-8416

ICCFA.com

International Conference of Funeral Service Examining Boards
Provides information on regulations and oversees complaints.

1885 Shelby Lane, Fayetteville, AR 72704

Phone: 479-442.7076 / Fax: 479-442.7090

info@theconferenceonline.org

TheConferenceOnline.org/contact.shtml

The Jewish Funeral Directors of America, Inc.
The JFDA is an international association of funeral homes who predominantly serve members of the Jewish faith.

Seaport Landing, 150 Lynnway, Suite 506, Lynn, MA 01902

Phone 781-477-9300 / Fax 781-477-9393

JFDA.org/about.html / info@jfda.org

National Funeral Directors Association
13625 Bishop's Drive, Brookfield, WI 53005

Toll-free: 800-228-6332 / Phone: 262-789-1880 / Fax: 262-789-6977

E-mail: nfda@nfda.org **NFDA.org**

National Funeral Directors & Morticians Association, Inc.

Traditionally an association of African-American funeral directors.

3951 Snapfinger Parkway, # 570 Omega World Center, Decatur, GA 30035

Toll-free: 800-434-0958 / Fax: 404-286-6573

NFDMA.com

Quaker Faith and Practices
Link to a PDF on Death, Dying, and Bereavement Faith and Practice by the Southeastern Yearly Meeting.

SEYM.org/FP.pdf/DyingDeathBereavement.pdf

United Network for Organ Sharing
Assists transplant doctors, patients, and members of the public by helping to ensure that organs are procured and distributed in a fair and timely manner.

700 North 4th Street, Richmond, VA 23219

Phone: 888-894-6361

UNOS.org/default.asp

Bibliography

BOOKS

Carlson, Lisa. *Caring for the Dead: Your Final Act of Love*. Hinesburg, VT: Upper Access, 1997.

Clifford, Denis. *Plan Your Estate*. Berkeley, CA: NOLO, 2008.

Cochrane, Don S. *Simply Essential Funeral Planning Kit*. Bellingham, WA: Self-Counsel Press, 2002.

Harris, Mark. *Grave Matters: A Journey through the Modern Funeral Industry to a Natural Way of Burial*. New York: Scribner, 2007, 2008.

Kubler-Ross, Elizabeth. *On Death and Dying*. New York: First Collier Books Trade, 1993.

Morgan, Earnest. *Dealing Creatively with Death: A Manual of Death Education and Simple Burial*. Hinesberg, VT: Upper Access, 2001.

Norrgard, Lee E., and Jo Demars. *Final Choices: Making End-Of-Life Decisions*. Santa Barbara, CA: ABC-Clio, 1992.

Siegel, Mark A. (editor), Jacquelyn Quiram (editor), Nancy R Jacobs (editor). *Profile of the Nation: An American Portrait*. Wylie, TX: Information Plus, 1998.

MAGAZINES

Alexander, Max. "Which Way Out." *Smithsonian Magazine*, March 2009.

Barker, Beth and Karen Reyes. "R.I.P. Off." *Modern Maturity*, March–April 2000.

"Hitting 60." *Newsweek*, November 14, 2005.

"It Must Be True." *The Week*, November 11, 2005.

Levine, Gary. "Spotlight, News a Glance." *The Week*, May 26, 2006.

Popescu, Roxana. "Thinking Outside The Urn." *Newsweek*, November 12, 2007.

NEWSPAPERS

The Associated Press. "Funeral Home Will Store Your DNA Legacy." *The Daily Press*, June 22, 2006.

Guy, Mike. "The Remix; GRAVE MATTERS | Parting Glass." *The New York Times*, October 9, 2005.

Harris, Melissa. "Families Turn to the Web to Grieve." *The Baltimore Sun*, February 23, 2007.

O'Connell, Loraine. "Company Turns Coffins into Artistic Canvases." *The Orlando Sentinel*, The Daily Press, January 15, 2000.

Selvin, Joel. "Grateful Dead Star Jerry Garcia Dies at Treatment Center." *San Francisco Chronicle*, August 14, 1995.

Toosi, Nahal. "Remember '05? E-mail Can Jog Memory." The Associated Press.

Vegh Steven G., "Memorial Forests." *The Virginian Pilot*, September 28, 2008.

PUBLICATIONS

The Funeral Consumers Alliance of Tidewater. "Putting My House In Order," "Probate in Virginia," "Comparison Charts of Funeral Home Rates and Discount Providers."

WEBSITES

AARP Education & Outreach. "Identity theft." AARP. April 8, 2009. http://www.aarp.org/money/consumer/articles/WiseConsumerIdentityTheft.html

Beyer, Gerry W. "Body Disposition—The Aussie Way." Wills, Trusts & Estates Prof Blog. February 26, 2008. http://lawprofessors.typepad.com/trusts_estates_prof/2008/02/body-dispositio.html

Brown, Patricia Leigh. "Eco-Friendly Burial Sites Give a Chance to Be Green Forever." *The New York Times*. August 13, 2005. http://www.nytimes.com/2005/08/13/national/13cemetery.html?_r=1

Carlson, Lisa. "Funerals - Home Burial." All Experts. August 10, 2004. http://en.allexperts.com/q/Funerals-1739/home-burial.htm

Cox, Rachel S. "A Movement to Grief Back Home Many Bereaved Opting to Bypass Funeral Industry." *The Washington Post*. June 5, 2005. http://www.washingtonpost.com/wp-dyn/content/article/2005/06/04/AR2005060401667.html

Dizikes, Cynthia. "'Death Midwife as Funeral Alternative." *Los Angeles Times*. December 26, 2008. http://articles.latimes.com/2008/dec/26/nation/na-at-home-funerals26

Editors of Publications International, Ltd. "9 Strange Last Wills and Testaments." How Stuff Works. http://people.howstuffworks.com/9-strange-last-wills-and-testaments.htm

Thalia, "Famous Gravestone Quotes." *Emule*, October 3, 2003.

"Key Points Outlining WHY HOUSE BILL 1202 SHOULD BE TABLED." Natural Transitions. http://www.naturaltransitions.org/

Obituary Guide. http://www.obituaryguide.com/template.php

Pitz, Marylynne. "Eternally Green: Woodland Burials Are a Natural Alternative to an Embalmed Afterlife." *Pittsburgh Post-Gazette*. January 30, 2008. http://www.post-gazette.com/pg/08030/853146-51.stm

Unique Funeral Products. Various pages listing memorial products. http://www.uniquefuneralproducts.com/blog/category/memorial-products/

VanderKnyff, Rick. "The Basics Scammed—Even After You Die." MSN. 2009. http://moneycentral.msn.com/content/Banking/FinancialPrivacy/P124147.asp

Glossary

accession A process used to accept, by purchase, gift, or trade, items for a museum's collection.

body bequeathing Donating one's body for science and research.

body farm A forensic anthropology center that studies human decomposition

burial The ritual of placing a person or object into the ground.

burial, home The burial of your body on private property you own.

burial liner. A strongbox covering only the top and sides of the coffin; used to protect coffin from with weight of the earth and cemetery equipment.

burial at sea The disposing of human remains in the ocean, normally from a ship or boat.

burial vault A strong, sealed box designed to protect the enclosed coffin; used primarily to protect the coffin from the weight of the earth and cemetery equipment.

cadaver A dead body.

carbon footprint. The sum of all of CO_2 (carbon dioxide) emissions produced by your activities in a given time frame.

cemetery An area set apart for, or containing, graves, tombs, or funeral urns; a graveyard; a churchyard; a necropolis.

coffin A box or case in which the body of a dead person is placed for burial; also called a casket.

columbarium A sepulchral vault or other structure having recesses in the walls to hold urns.

commercial cemetery A cemetery that is a for-profit business.

committal service A small service with only family and close friends attending; usually held at the graveside before the body is buried or at the crematory before the actual cremation.

conservation burial ground A cemetery dedicated to ecological restoration and landscape-level conservation; has an established conservation organization as a long-term warden.

cord blood stem cells Stem cells harvested from the umbilical cord.

cremains The remains of a dead body after cremation.

cremation The incineration of a dead body using heat, vaporization, and flame to reduce the body to its basic elements.

cremation coffin A casket meeting cremation requirements, generally made entirely of wood or wood by-products.

cremation, direct Cremation without a viewing or funeral service, using the minimum type of container.

cremation society A group, not necessarily a nonprofit, designed to help members obtain the best financial deal for a funeral through advance planning.

cremation, traditional Where the funeral home or crematorium picks up the body, takes care of all of the paperwork, and presides over the entire process.

crematorium A furnace where a corpse can be burned and reduced to ashes.

cremulator A machine that pulverizes cremated remains into the appearance of grains of sand.

cryonics The use of ultra-cold temperature to preserve the human body with the intent of restoring good health when technology becomes available.

crypt An underground vault, chamber, or cellar used as a burial chamber; also a vault in a mausoleum.

death benefits Money paid to the beneficiary of the deceased; includes U.S. Social Security insurance, other insurance, and annuities.

death certificate A legal paper signed by a doctor, medical examiner, or coroner certifying date, time and cause of death, and other vital statistical data pertaining to the deceased.

direct disposition The removal of the body from place of death, placing it into a container or casket, and delivering it to the cemetery or crematorium without any attendant religious services or other rites or ceremonies.

death notice A listing announcing a person's death by giving such minimal information as time and date of service; much shorter than an obituary.

eco-forests Land where cremated remains are placed beside a leased, memorial tree.

embalming The preservation of a human body with preservatives in order to prevent decay and to forestall decomposition.

eulogy A speech or written tribute praising someone who has died.

executor The person appointed either by the deceased or by the court to administer an estate.

family cemetery A cemetery located on private land.

Federal Trade Commission An independent agency of the United States government that promotes consumer protection and the prevention of anti-competitive business practices.

Forensic Anthropology Center at Texas State University A facility located in San Marcos, Texas, that researches problems related to outdoor crime scenes and decomposition rates for human remains under various topographical and climate conditions.

Forensic Anthropology Center at the University of Tennessee A facility located outside of Knoxville, Tennessee, that uses forensic anthropology to study human decomposition.

Funeral Consumers Alliance The oldest and largest national non-profit funeral consumer advocacy organization in the country.

funeral obituary An announcement of a person's death, explaining when and where the funeral took place.

funeral A ceremony at which a dead person is buried or cremated.

grave A single burial space; a place for the burial of a corpse.

green burial Often called "natural burial," where the body is prepared for burial without the use of chemical preservatives, is put into a biodegradable container, and is placed in the earth to decompose naturally.

green caskets Coffins made from fully biodegradable products that are free from varnish, plastic, metal, toxic glue, oil, or animal products.

green urn Urns made from natural substances that are biodegradable, non-toxic, environmentally safe, and dissolve completely in water.

intestate Dying without having made a legally valid will.

interment The final disposition of remains by entombment, burial, or placement in a niche.

lawn crypt Often referred to as "underground mausoleum"; lots situated on a raised area of land, where both single- and double-depth crypts are pre-installed in the ground.

marrow Soft tissue found in the interior cavities of bones. A major site of blood cell production and which contains stem cells.

mausoleum A free-standing building constructed as a monument, holding spaces for interment.

memorial marker A marker used to identify a grave or urn placement; also used to identify a place where ashes were scattered, or to commemorate the location of the deceased.

memorial reefs Marine habitats for fish and other forms of sea life constructed from or containing cremated remains.

memorial service A service held without the body present; usually dedicated to the memory of the deceased.

memorial society A nonprofit consumer group run by members whose purpose is to help members obtain the best financial deal for a funeral through advance planning.

national cemetery A cemetery owned by the government and used for the internment of veterans and their dependents.

natural burial ground A cemetery that protects nature, does not intrude on the landscape, and forgoes the use of irrigation, pesticides, and herbicides.

neuropreservation In cryonics, relating to preservation of the brain only.

obituary A notice, usually in a newspaper, that announces a person's death and includes an extended account of the person's life and list of family members.

organ donation Removal of the tissues or organs from a person who has recently died, or from a living donor, for the purpose of transplanting.

OPTN The Organ Procurement and Transplantation Network A unified transplant network established by the United States Congress under the National Organ Transplant Act (NOTA) of 1984, linking all professionals involved in the donation and transplantation system.

pallbearer An individual, usually family or close friend, whose duty it is to carry the casket at necessary times.

pallbearer, honorary An individual whose position in the funeral procession is close to the casket, but who does not carry the casket or coffin.

peripheral blood stem cells Stem cells from bone marrow pushed out into the blood stream by injections of medication and then harvested.

pillow marker A type of memorial monument that has the back side higher than the front, giving the granite a sloped effect, making the lettering and design much easier to view.

plot An area in a cemetery that has more than one grave.

preneed The payment for a funeral prior to death.

probate The process of establishing that a document, such as a will, is genuine legal and valid.

public nonprofit cemetery A cemetery owned and operated by the city or county.

real property Property in the form of houses and land, as opposed to personal possessions.

religious cemetery A cemetery owned by a religious group and used specifically for the internment of member of that religion or faith.

retort A vessel where substances are distilled or decomposed by heat.

Southeast Texas Applied Forensic Science Facility at Sam Houston State University A facility adjacent to the Sam Houston State Forest near Huntsville, Texas, designed to advance academic and technical knowledge in the application of forensic science disciplines to crime scenes and criminal activities.

Uniform Donor Card A commonly used document signifying an individual's intent to designate donation of his organs for transplantation upon his death.

urn A vase with a footed base into which cremated remains are placed.

veteran A member of the Armed Forces: Army, Navy, Air Force, Marine Corps, or Coast Guard.

viewing A vigil held over a corpse the night before burial, usually with the casket present and open.

visitation A vigil held before the funeral, where the immediate family is gathered to receive condolences from extended family, friends and acquaintances.

wake Another form of visitation but more informal, often involving food, drink, and storytelling.

water resolution Alkaline hydrolysis: a process using heated water, pressure, and alkalinity to accelerate natural decomposition, leaving a liquid that can be dried into a form resembling ashes.

Western Carolina Human Identification Laboratory A facility located at Western Carolina University in Cullowhee, North Carolina, that is dedicated to the recovery, storage, and analysis of human remains.

will A legal document that declares your wishes concerning distribution of your property and assets, and the care of any minor children after you die.

will, holographic A handwritten will without the presence of witnesses; only recognized by a few states and it rarely holds up in court.

will, living States your wishes regarding medical care concerning life support should you become debilitated.

will, oral A spoken testament made before a witness that is only recognized in a few states under a few rare circumstances.

will, self-proving/testamentary A formally prepared document that is signed in the presence of witnesses and abides by all state rules and regulations.

will, valid A will that is accepted by the court.

will, video A video made in which the deceased reads his properly executed will and explains why he left what to whom.

Index

Greek Orthodox 49
green burial 11, 28, 75
Green Burial Council 32, 33
Green Burial Council Conservation
     Burial Grounds 32
green burial ground 67, 70
green burial grounds 98
green burial movement 28, 73, 84
green burial resource center 40
green burial site 62
green burial sites 33, 59
Green Casket Company 74
Green caskets 72
green cemeteries 81, 83
green cemetery 84
green coffin 79
green coffins 72
Green Daily 50
green or natural burial 20
greens urns 84
green urn 84
grief 147, 148, 150, 152
GriefNet 153
Grief Observed, A 152
Grief Recovery Handbook, The 152
Grief Relief Resource 150
GriefShare 153
Grief Support Services.Org 154
ground level markers 27
Guardian, The 60
guest book 105

H

hair 106
Hall, Julie 141
Halloween 65
Hammett, Dashiell 98
Handel 93
Harley-Davidson 42
Harris, Mark 31
Harvard Medical School 153
headstone 26, 123

headstones 121
healing 38
*Healing After Loss: Daily Meditations
     For Working Through Grief* 152
health department 39
health department rules 35
hearing loss 7
Hearse 22
heart valves 6
Heathrow Airport 60
hepatitis 5
herbicides 29
Hickman, Martha W. 152
Hickok, Wild Bill 123
HIV 5
"Hokey Pokey, The" 65
Holly, Buddy 121
Holographic Will 133
home burial 11, 20, 75
home burial requirements 39
home funeral 40
Home Funeral Directory 40
home funerals 38
home preparation 11
Homer 48
home service 11, 51
home services 12
Home site 122
home sites 121
Honey Creek Woodlands 33
hospice 146
Hourglass urn 82
"How to Build a Potato Gun" 63
"How to Perform a Pagan Funeral" 98
"How to Plan a Christian Funeral" 94
"How To Plan A Funeral" 14
"How to Plan an Affordable Funeral" 14
"How to prepare food for a funeral
     reception" 110
human remains 4
Huntsville 3, 6
Huntsville, Texas 3
hymns 100

About the Author

Author, broadcast journalist, and freelance writer Karen Jones is the author of the novel *Kingdom of Hearts* and coauthor of *Up the Bestseller Lists*, which offers hands-on advice and guerilla techniques for authors who want to aggressively and successfully promote and market their work.

Jones has fifteen years of experience in television news at ABC-affiliate WVEC in Norfolk, Virginia, as an on-air anchor and feature reporter. She directed the Virginia Writers Conference for five years, was an advisor for the Bay School for the Arts, and is a member of the National League of American Pen Women and the Authors Guild.

Jones has taught writing workshops and seminars at Louisiana State University, Austin Peay University, and Old Dominion University and she has taught courses in romance novel writing at the University of Richmond and Christopher Newport University. She currently teaches week-long writing camps on Ocracoke Island, North Carolina.

She can be reached through her web site: **DeathForBeginners.com**.